M000082880

ESTÉE LAUDER

ALSO BY THE SAME AUTHOR

Kilgallen: A Biography of Dorothy Kilgallen
Miss Tallulah Bankhead

ESTÉE LAUDER
BEYOND THE MAGIC

AN UNAUTHORIZED BIOGRAPHY BY

LEE ISRAEL

MACMILLAN PUBLISHING COMPANY   New York

Copyright © 1985 by Carthage, Inc.

All rights reserved. No part of this book may be reproduced or
transmitted in any form or by any means, electronic or mechanical,
including photocopying, recording or by any information storage and
retrieval system, without permission in writing from the Publisher.

Macmillan Publishing Company
866 Third Avenue, New York, N.Y. 10022
Collier Macmillan Canada, Inc.

Library of Congress Catalog Card Number: 85-24131

Macmillan books are available at special discounts
for bulk purchases for sales promotions, premiums,
fund-raising, or educational use.
For details, contact:
Special Sales Director
Macmillan Publishing Company
866 Third Avenue
New York, N.Y. 10022

10   9   8   7   6   5   4   3   2   1

Printed in the United States of America

CONTENTS

ACKNOWLEDGMENTS

The following are the people who made *Estée Lauder: Beyond the Magic* possible. The list would double at least were I authorized to reveal the names of all my sources, many of whom made extremely significant contributions to the book. For a variety of understandable reasons, however, they chose to talk without attribution.

There were numbers of people, especially in Estée's own family, whose cooperation I earnestly solicited. They chose to withhold their assistance.

I am especially indebted to Laurie Thompson, whiz in the areas of genealogy, through whose incredible expertise I was able to obtain and understand documents for which I would not even have known to search. The Amelia Bassin files on the current history of fragrance and cosmetics were very helpful, as were her insights and overview of the beauty business. Lucille Carlan Rottkov gave me hours of recollections on the John Schotz story and massive documentation. Jane Abbott, Director of the Oconomowoc Historical Society Museum, labored long investigating the Estée Lauder ties in her area; Vincent J. Tomeo helped similarly in Corona.

These are the people who helped me to see and hear Estée Lauder: Diane L. Ackerman; Agnes Ash (who also opened the files of *The Palm Beach Daily News* to me); Marvin Davis; Harry Doyle; Bob Fiske; Lois Hagen; Florian Harvat; Ancky Johnson;

Joe LaRosa; Anthony Liebler; Andrew Lucarelli; Allan G. Mottus; Arthur Noto; Mary Sanford.

I am grateful to the following people for their contributions: Jody Abramson; Ann Anderson; Michele Anish; Jean Baer; Helen Baum; Marilyn Bender; Carter Bennett; Clifford Berger; Ed Beyler; Mrs. Samuel Bloom; Kim Bodden; Helene Bogarte; Larry Borston; James Brady; Mr. and Mrs. Alan Carlan; Joe Carney; Ken Cobb; Max Cuck; Charlotte Curtis; Renee Daniels; Don Davis; Paulette Debruille; Aida DeMaris; Jeffrey Dymowski; Edna L. Emma; Anthony Federici; Rudy Ferrara; Sara Fredericks; M. Furer; Betty Furness; Joseph Giordano; Mrs. Gleiberman; Martha Gordon; Virginia Graham; Dr. Leo Hershkowitz, Jean Isobe; Harry Kess; Dr. Albert M. Kligman; Dr. Robert Kramer; Helen S. Latner; Jesse Levy; Joan Lowry; Everett G. McDonough; George McManus; Linda Mesiano; Janine Metz; Frederic Morton; Sidell Mundell; Harry Murray; Ralph Naccarato; Pauline Ney; Mary Obolensky; Martin Pomerence; Tom Poster; David Pratt; Mary Presper; Eileen Ryan; Richard B. Salomon; Mrs. R. Schapiro; Nina Schick; Gertrude Sheldon; Mr. Shipman; Irma Shorell; Sidney R. Silverman; Liz Smith, Henry Spira; Mark Staples; Molly Staub; Mac Stern; Jean Towell; Don Viall; Jeanette Vitkin; Cynthia Watkin; Anna White; Bob Wirtz; and Jerry Wressler.

With special thanks to Robert Stewart, my wonderful, tireless editor, and to Gloria Safier, agent and old friend.

ESTÉE LAUDER

INTRODUCTION

The world is fragrant and rich, impeccable in taste and tone. The woman who moves easefully here is a flawless, almost glacial beauty, perhaps southern, perhaps WASP, and comfortable anywhere. The objects that surround her are a reflection of a pedigree as glowing as her complexion. There are background and cheekbones and indolent summers. She has been to the best schools. Her children are bilingual and well mannered. A single calla lily sits in her Ming vase; her guests are fascinating; her table is perfect. Her environment is an extension of her own elegance and eclecticism. She's Tuesday's child grown up amidst topiaries or magnolias.

She is the Estée Lauder woman, the most famous of whom was model Karen Graham. She has come to represent in allure and glamour the vast cosmetics company that was founded by Estée Lauder in 1947. The life-style that Karen Graham projected, and her successors continue to project, is kindred in spirit to the life-style for which Estée herself has come to be known.

The reigning queen of the class-marketed cosmetics company, Estée, now seventy-seven, owns mansions in the south of France, Palm Beach, and New York City. She has been decorated with the French Legion of Honor. She is a close friend of First Lady Nancy Reagan. She has entertained and been entertained by the Duke and Duchess of Windsor, Grace Kelly, Mrs. Frank Jay Gould, Mary Lasker, and the Begum Aga Khan.

The very name—Estée Lauder—has come to signify glamour, exclusivity, and an insistent social cachet. She once explained that cachet in a two-page *Women's Wear Daily* profile in September 1969: "You never start without anything," Estée told *WWD*'s reporter, Toni Kosover. "If you are something, it is always the result of something in your background."

Estée elaborated on that background, referring, almost reverentially, to her parents: her "Hungarian-Viennese mother" who regularly visited the spas of Europe and never went out without a parasol and a pair of gloves; her Czechoslovakian father, a horseman and landowner. Estée talked of her education, which began formally on Long Island and finished, informally, during the frequent trips she took abroad with her mother and her sister, Grace Shepard.

Then she evoked for *WWD* the birth of her beauty dream. The article relates, "She was 12-years-old and living with her family in Flushing, L.I., in a large private house with a stable, a chauffeured car and an Italian nurse, when she began thinking seriously about becoming a skin doctor." The dream was apparently induced by the arrival of her mother's brother, "a Viennese chemist called Dr. John Schatz," who came to live with her family during World War I: " 'We built a white laboratory for him right next to the stables. I spent hours in there working with him. It fascinated me.

" 'Mine is hardly a rags to riches story,' " Estée asserted, sitting in a Second Empire chair, wearing an original Ungaro, and sipping champagne in her lavish offices overlooking Central Park. She told of having had "many royal visitors" to her father's home in Flushing. She then pointed to a picture taken of herself that she claimed had appeared in the rotogravure society section of *The New York Times* when she married Joseph Lauder in 1930. Estée added, " 'Bernice Chrysler's picture was on the same page. She was marrying Edward Garbish [*sic*] at the same time Joe and I were getting married.' "

Such details as the cosmetics queen offered that day to the fortunate journalist are *extremely* rare. Although Estée has been in the public eye for about three decades, there is overall a unique thinness, almost a porosity to the story of her life that she has told.

Considering this stretch of thirty years, one is struck by the odd landscaping of the story. It's barren, almost lunar. The oddment is this: In all the interviews, statements, press releases, and column items, there is, to start with, an almost total absence of *dates*. Ironically, despite the admission to *WWD* that her marriage to Joseph Lauder occurred in 1930, the reference to her picture appearing in the rotogravure section with Bernice Chrysler only confuses the issue.

This datelessness pervades everything. She does not give her date of birth, not even a birthday. (Bernice Chrysler, however, *was* married to Edgar William Garbisch at St. Bartholomew's Church on Saturday, January 4, 1930. A two-column picture of her, in a princess gown of heavy white satin carrying a sheaf of calla lillies, appeared in the Sunday *Times* rotogravure section. No picture of Estée has been found. In fact, Estée's marriage certificate is dated January 15, 1930—eleven days *after* the Chrysler wedding.) And there is certainly no mention of her *second* marriage to husband Joseph. You can't find out exactly when her two boys were born. A date is disclosed only when it is already in the public domain, such as the formation of her first company, the Estée Lauder Cosmetic Company, in 1947 (which is frequently told as 1946); such as the debut of her sensational fragrance, Youth-Dew, in 1953.

Beyond this odd lacuna, Estée will not name names. Early on, it somehow became known that her maiden name was Mentzer; so she was compelled to live with that. But she nowhere reveals the names of her *parents*. Three or four times, in some comparatively in-depth piece, she mentions her mother. She does a short, almost cinematic litany about that mother: a quick take is

3

all you get. And they are all little beauty tableaux: "Mother said to me, 'You brushed my hair twice today' "; "In Milwaukee, a woman came in every day just to brush my mother's hair"; "My mother was so beautiful a man fifteen years younger married her."

But mother is given no name; neither is father. Her father was younger than her mother, but not by fifteen years, as she claims. Is the man Estée refers to her mother's previous husband—whose existence is known only to members of the family? It would seem unlikely, unless he sired his first child at six, which is young even for a Hungarian.

Estée is utterly uncompromising about not revealing their names. It is customary, for instance, among New Yorkers, to mark the passing of a parent by taking a small space on the obituary page of *The New York Times*: a couple of lines that inform about the death, which typically include decedent's name, place of interment, and a list of survivors of the immediate family. This Estée did not do when her mother died in Mohegan, New York, on August 23, 1957 at the age of eighty-six. Neither did she do it when her father died, at eighty-two, in 1962. She was not estranged from them; indeed, she was a loving and dutiful daughter.

By the time of her father's death, Estée's Mentzer identity had been made public. But not the names Rose and Max Mentzer. Nor had she uttered one public word about a passel of half-brothers named Rosenthal. Had she made a declaration of bereavement on the passing of either parent, she would have provided a link to her real past; those facts would have belied the legend she had begun to weave and made unseemly trouble.

Canny as Estée is, she has never been consistent. Marilyn Bender, a business reporter for *The New York Times*, tried as assiduously as any other writer to determine some truth beyond the Estée Lauder presentation. Bender finally had to settle on confusion rather than substance as her theme. She wrote in her book *At the Top*, published in 1975, in a chapter called "Estée Lauder: A Family Affair":

Tales of childhood in Milwaukee interchanged with anecdotes about Scranton, giving rise to reports that she was a coal miner's daughter, which she denied. A member of her family once divulged that her formative years were passed on the frontier where the borough of Queens meets Nassau County on Long Island. A beauty editor who recounted her own Sicilian background to Estée Lauder at lunch one day came away convinced that Estée Lauder was half Italian and convent-bred. Mrs. Lauder was mistress of the throw-away diversionary remark. "They're old Tiffany and belonged to my mother in Vienna," she announced within earshot of a *Women's Wear Daily* reporter who was attending a dinner in the Lauder Manhattan chateau. Mother's alleged possessions were silver soup plates and matching service plates displayed at one of Estée's little dinners for twenty-two. For those who enjoy watching social climbers maneuver up the rocky slopes to acceptance, Estée's act was no less entrancing than that of a marine scaling a crag during an exhibition of guerrilla survival training.

Earl Blackwell wrote in his *Celebrity Register*, in 1973, that obtaining information on this "Viennese-born luminary . . . is akin to penetrating a stone wall with a needle."

Virginia Graham, the television personality, has known Estée since Estée's stint behind a counter at an East Side Manhattan beauty salon. About Estée's background, Graham exclaims, "I don't think the FBI knows!"

What was she telling and to whom? Obviously, she was telling, or at least Blackwell was believing, that she was born in Vienna, Austria. *Who's Who* for 1976–1977 lists her birthplace as Vienna; though by the 1982–1983 edition, that formidable reference work, which prints information provided by the subject, has her born in New York City. An early story that ran in *The World-Telegram* in 1962, and which appears to have been based on an actual interview with Estée, places her birth in Flushing,

Queens, "of French-Viennese parents" and goes on to assert that she travels a great deal: "She has in fact been traveling since the day she packed her bags to study dermatology in Vienna." She told the *Palm Beach Daily News* that her father was Viennese and in the social register, and never had to work.

Then there is a whole biographical oeuvre that places Estée in the Milwaukee area, with an emphasis on the beautiful old ivied and Episcopal lake district of Oconomowoc-Delafield-Waukesha. This yarn goes back to the late forties. She was *not* inventing out of whole cloth; rather she was making little fish like big whales speak. Estée was then living on West End Avenue ("too many people think I started my business in my kitchen on West End Avenue with a jar of homemade face cream," she complained to the *Palm Beach Daily News* in 1971). Eileen Ryan, who was a reporter with *The Milwaukee Journal*, visited Estée because she had heard Estée was a hometown girl: "When I saw her for the first time," Ryan recounts, "she was living in a very sparsely furnished, very ordinary apartment on West End Avenue. And she told me, 'Oh, I know Milwaukee well because I lived in Oconomowoc.' And she was vague about it. When I asked her when she had lived there, she said, 'Oh, that's some time ago.' "

Lois Hagen, also of the *Journal*, interviewed Estée when the latter was about to accept an award from Gimbel's Milwaukee that was given annually to distinguished Wisconsinites. Hagen wrote: "Mrs. Lauder grew up in Milwaukee and 'lived there so many years that I still think of it as home. I went through grade school there and spent my vacations at our summer house in Delafield, near St. John's Academy. After my mother moved to New York, she continued to return to Delafield every summer until her death, and I, too, have returned many times.' "

In fact, Estée does have a Milwaukee history, some of which is and some of which is not determinable. Her mother's sister, Sarah Gottlieb, lived in the area. But here is another example of the throw-away diversionary remark, true in substance but not in

6

implication. Oconomowoc, in the last part of the nineteenth century, became known as the Newport of the West. In the twenties and thirties, it was the playground of the rich-rich from Chicago, St. Louis, and Milwaukee. Nestled between two beautiful lakes, Oconomowoc means "River of Falling Waters." Beyond that, to anyone familiar with the area, it connotes chic parties, polo, lavishly landscaped grounds. *The Heritage Trail Guidebook*, which describes the area, boasts: "Where else in the States can one look across a lake and see 'summer cottages' equaling the grandeur of European castles?" It was a place where rich Christian parents sent rich Christian young women to find rich Christian young men. St. John's is an Episcopal Military Seminary, a place of Gothic archways and privilege, and snappy uniformed cadets.

Sarah Gottlieb did have a small house there that was really a cottage. It was set back from a lake that was visible through the kitchen window. It was five minutes by car from St. John's. Sarah died in 1953, impoverished; she paid for her mortgage and for the small jobs that had to be done around her house by swapping the lovely linens and dishes she had brought over from Budapest and by bartering the delicate embroidery called matjo she had learned to do in Hungary.

As a young girl Estée undoubtedly did visit her aunt. But Sarah's unheated little summer house, set back from Lake Nagawicka, was not one of the Bavarian castles. And if Estée remembers the Academy, it is because she probably attended a dance or two there in the gymnasium.

The truth is that Estée was *in* but not *of* Oconomowoc. That was a romantic world of riches and promises and dreams: a far better thing than she was living. And no doubt it was what she aspired to. She was like Jay Gatsby gazing across the lake at the green light at the end of Daisy's dock.

1

BEGINNINGS

She was born Josephine Esther Mentzer on July 1, 1908, on Hillside Avenue in Corona, Queens. She was born at home, delivered by a midwife, which was the custom in Corona. She was the ninth and last child of Rose Schotz Rosenthal Mentzer and Max Mentzer. Two children had died before Josephine Esther's birth. She had one full sister, Grace, who was two years older. The five other children were all products of her mother's first marriage to an Abraham Rosenthal. Josephine was apparently named after her maternal grandmother, who was called Pepi, the Hungarian nickname for Josephine. Pepi was married to an Izi Schatz.

Very little is ascertainable about Rose, the mother whose hair her youngest daughter loved to fix. Like her sister Sarah Gottlieb, she was born in Hungary. She was twenty-nine years old when she arrived in New York City by way of Hamburg on the S.S. *Palatia* on August 5, 1898. She had in tow five children when she made the twelve-day voyage: Bertha, nine (a relative claimed she died in a fire before Estée's birth); Marcus, seven; Sandor, six; Isidor, four; and Jeno, two. Her husband, Abraham Rosenthal, had come over first, undoubtedly to establish himself and prepare the way. The *Palatia's* register has her last residence in Satoraljaujhely, which is in the northern part of Hungary, near the Czech border. It states further that she and Bertha could read and write; that her religion was "Hebrew." On the day of her arrival, showers were cooling off a city that had sweltered the day before. Several people had died from the heat. There had been a riot in the Brownsville section of Brooklyn, in the teeming Jewish community, touched off by a young Jewish girl's perception that her public school teacher had attempted to convert her.

Nothing is known of the husband Rose was coming to join. However, divorce was virtually unthinkable then. The strong probability is that he died, though desertion was not unknown in the boiling immigrant experience.

Since it has been observed that in those days most first births occurred two years after marriage, it may be assumed from the fact that Grace was born in 1906, that Rose Schotz married Max Mentzer circa 1904. Unfortunately, no record of that marriage is discoverable.

Max Mentzer was also a native of Hungary. The name Mentzer means "the Jew from Mainz." He was born, according to his naturalization papers, in March of 1878, though his death certificate gives his birth date as 1881; this last is probably the more accurate date. To apply for naturalization, an immigrant had to be at least twenty-one. And he claimed to be twenty-one in the papers filed in 1902. It is not unlikely that he added three years to his age in order to qualify. Assuming he was born in 1881, he was only thirteen when he arrived in New York. His profession on the naturalization papers was given as tailor; his residence, 91 Lewis Street, which was the Lower East Side. The man who swore to his moral character was a cigar dealer, Israel Bergido.

On the papers, Max was spelling his last name "Mentczer"; he would simplify the spelling to Mentzer by the time of his first daughter's birth. Max's nativity is given only as Hungarian. When he died, his daughter, Estée, was the informant. She listed his birthplace as Czechoslovakia. This being a no more prestigious nativity than Hungary—indeed, it would have been less esteemed in Estée's view—veracity may be assumed. It might mean that Max hailed from a part of Hungary that would be absorbed by Czechoslovakia by 1957.

Placing him there, and considering the varieties of Hungarian transliteration, it may well be that Estée's father was at least a cousin to the "Menczer" family to whom writer Frederic Morton is related. Morton traveled extensively within Hungary to research his relatives, and he used them as a model for the family he names Varungy in his recently published novel, *The Forever Street*. Those Menczers came from Holice. Morton recounts, "Holice is now in Slovakia, but it was part of Hungary for a long time. It's near Bratislava; and it's very close to the place where the Austrian-Czech-Hungarian borders meet."

In the course of his research, Morton discovered that all of his relatives had misrepresented themselves; He visited the Jewish cemetery in the town they pretended to come from, but he found no Menczers there. "It was a shock I had," Morton says. "They had all pretended to have been from a bigger and more important village . . . But they were all very rural rather than mercantile: one of those Jewish families that was neither rabbinical nor mercantile. I remember how much my grandmother loved the country. That was true of many of the families that came from that Hungarian corner of Slovakia. The vast majority of them raised geese and force fed the geese for pâté de foie gras."

Morton speculated that Max could have been "at least a cousin" to Joseph Menczer. Joseph Menczer was a Bronx jeweler who had been born in Hungary in 1890, one of about thirteen children. He left Hungary in high dudgeon when his father slapped him across the face for showing up late at a family gathering. "My grandfather slapped him, he walked out, and applied for a visa," Morton recounts. In May 1920, Joseph was under investigation on five counts of grand larceny involving the illegal disposition of $100,000 worth of jewelry. He absconded to Canada, but he was arrested in a railroad depot in Montreal. A

10

New York detective recognized him from a "prominent pimple" on his forehead.

Whatever his relationship to the carbuncular jeweler, a rural predilection did manifest itself in the young Max Mentzer. He settled in Corona, which was at the time quite sylvan. When his two girls were born he was still tailoring, but he was to open a feed and grain establishment, which eventually became a hardware store, over which the Mentzer family lived. A neighborhood woman who grew up in Corona remembers Max as "rugged, big, rusty-color from the sun and the outdoors." He was nicknamed "Schotzy," which means "dear one" in Hungarian. And Rose? A Corona resident remembers: "The mother was, you know, one of the real mamas. A pretty little thing. She was not heavy, but she was bosomy and she had gray-black hair when I knew her. Well kept. I don't remember her looking anything like Estée.

"Mrs. Rosenthal's new husband was in hay and seed. Mentzer," she remembers. "My parents used to have horses and they used to get their hay and grain from them. My father used to send us to the store. He always made a fuss about children. Always a kind word and a pat on the head."

Estée's name must have derived from her middle name, Esther. No one remembers that she was ever called Josephine. There would come a time when she called herself Estelle. Her older sister Grace was called Renee. Her wedding invitation has the name spelled Renèe, with an accent grave, undoubtedly a grave error; the family called her *Ree*-Nee.

The Mentzer girls were among very, very few Jewish children in an almost entirely Italian neighborhood. Corona, which was once the eastern part of Elmhurst and the western part of Flushing, was named and settled in 1876 by a developer named Benjamin Hitchcock, who beckoned Italian immigrants there from the Lower East Side. Corona meant "the crown community." It was only two years before Estée's birth that the Queensboro Bridge was built connecting Corona with Manhattan seven miles away. When Estée was growing up, the streets were unpaved; most of the Italians who settled there had factory jobs; and the place smelled horrifically.

Corona was used as a dumping ground for raw garbage from the neighboring boroughs. The Brooklyn Ash Company spilled its refuse there from the side of railroad cars. The heaped cinders were called "Corona Mountain." Barges of manure were brought in from New York City and tied to the neighborhood docks where farmers unloaded the fertilizer and carted it to their fields. In a letter to the Sunday New York *News*, published in 1975, ? Mrs. Cela Beldy wrote: "Growing up in Corona in the early 1900; laid the foundation for us to endure the tribulations of two World Wars and the Depression . . . Our parents were truly pioneers."

In *The Great Gatsby*, F. Scott Fitzgerald refers to Corona, circa 1922, as "the valley of ashes bounded on one side by a small foul river . . . a fantastic farm where ashes grow like wheat into ridges and hills and grotesque gardens; where ashes take the forms of houses and chimneys and rising smoke."

Since Estée refrained her whole life from speaking either of Corona or her girlhood there, little is known of her early existence. However, for the woman who would claim to have taught the American woman how to wear fragrance, there were no sweet smells of childhood.

She attended P.S. 14, a red-brick schoolhouse a couple of blocks from her father's store. She was there from February 1913, kindergarten, until she was graduated from 8B in June 1921. She received all A's in conduct, except in the fifth grade when she lapsed to a B-plus. Her work never fell below B. In eight years, she was late for school only twice.

What she dreamed, or read, is undeterminable. She will dig only so far into the recesses of her early ambitions. "I loved to make everyone up when I was young. My mother would say, 'You brushed my hair twice today.' I was always interested in people being beautiful—the hair, the face. I used to comb my sister-in-law Fannie's hair. I love to see people just walking or playing tennis, who look like they have a cared-for face."

One could surmise that this may have been the only avenue she could pursue to change the unloveliness of her environment. But there were role models, too. Not her sweet little mother, certainly, who was old beyond her years and reportedly underwent an early senility; Estée saved her china but took after her in no discernible way and eventually might have become a caretaker child. She may well have learned, however, from the examples set by her sister-in-law Fannie and by Fannie's older sister, Frieda. They were two bright and rather exceptional merchants who ran a store across from Max Mentzer's establishment. Fannie was eleven years older than Estée, pretty and short and chunky, married to Estée's older half-brother, Isidor. Frieda was four years older than Fannie, and also married to an Isidore, who had been a streetcar conductor. They were the former Leppel sisters. Their father Levi Leppel—after whom Estée would name her first son, Leonard—had begun as a Jewish peddler on New York's Lower East Side. He moved on up to Harlem, where the more successful peddlers became merchants and then, in 1909, out to Corona. His first dry goods stores was called Leppel's; and when the daughters and their somewhat recessive husbands took it over, during Estée's growing-up years, they called it Plafker & Rosenthal—a department store.

Fannie was a survivor of the notorious Triangle Fire of 1911, which killed more than one hundred young, mostly Jewish and Italian working girls who were trapped inside because the exit doors were locked to keep them from taking unauthorized breaks on the stairwells. Frieda was her sympathetic older sister who suffered from rickets and, like some people with similar handicaps, learned empathy and compassion. They built Plafker & Rosenthal into a department store that became known as "The Macy's of Corona."

Frieda's daughter, Gertrude Sheldon, is now a retired high school gym teacher. Though she would not consent to talk about her "Aunt Estée's life" (except to say, "we're all very proud of her"), she did agree to reminisce about Plafker & Rosenthal and the women who were responsible for its success. "They were the talented merchants in the family," she recalls. "They were uneducated, but they were smart," she recounts. "They learned to speak Neapolitan Italian as well as any of their customers. They sold everything including communion dresses, and they gave generously to the local church. They extended credit to their customers during hard times and they dunned no one. My mother was the softer. She used to do guidance outside the store before it opened at seven in the morning. The store was open seven in the morning until eleven at night, six-and-a-half days a week. She talked to the Jews in Yiddish and to the Italians in Italian. Aunt Fannie was busy. She was the push-push of the store. She was assertive; we don't say aggressive anymore. They were very exciting, very moral people."

Years after their deaths, the Leppel sisters and their store are highly regarded by the virtually unchanged, very stable Italian community. A local Corona woman who was interviewed by historian Vincent Tomeo for an oral history project, recalled the Jewish merchants of the twenties and thirties: "They all had businesses there on Corona Avenue . . . Hymowitz, a grocery store . . . Spaniers' bakery . . . Then they had the Leppels. They were married and their husbands helped them with the store . . . Leppels were different kinds of people. They were very good to the Italians. They used to trust them until they could afford to pay for their clothing. They never had to dun them for money . . . Everybody today still remembers the Leppels."

The Leppels and the Rosenthals and the Mentzers were like an extended family. They all bought a piece of land in Paramus, New Jersey, that would become, after the families sold it, Beth-El Cemetery. Gertrude Sheldon remembers horseback riding out there "among the dead" before the cemetery population became too dense. She rode with Max Mentzer and drank goat's milk with him. Though the family sold its interest in the property, Max would end his days as cemetery director of Beth-El, taking families to their loved ones' graves in a horse-drawn carriage.

It may be assumed that Estée took something away from Corona. Though Plafker & Rosenthal was nothing like the empire she would build in size or stature, she did witness the growth of a business enhanced by the industry and the talents of two women who troubled to learn the language and the mores of an essentially foreign clientele. Estée would not master Neapolitan Italian, but in her own way and on a mammoth scale, employing her almost supernal mercantile skills, the example of the Leppel sisters could not have been unheeded. Estée learned a foreign language and catered to a clientele whose language and mores *she* would eventually absorb.

2

VIENNESE WALTZ

Her obsessive secretiveness about growing up in a noisome, albeit friendly, Italian working-class neighborhood touches on an untapped and perhaps untappable turbulence in Estée. Given her desire to enter the beauty business, Estée had good reason to play down her background. Though the cornerstone of the cosmetics field in the twenties and thirties was the basic, utile, moisturizing skin cream, the romance was already in place. To sell a cream, you sold a dream; and Corona was nobody's idea of Beulah Land.

Even the most modestly priced, mass-produced cold creams were frequently advertised with royal imprimaturs. In 1927 Pond's Cold Cream and Vanishing Cream featured in its print advertising "the charming little personal crest" of Queen Marie of Roumania, with a picture of the queen and the endorsement: "Over two years ago, Her Majesty, writing from Bucharest, was pleased to permit the Pond's Extract Company to quote her words expressing her faith in the efficacy of Pond's Two Creams." A subsequent letter, written in February 1925, says: "Her Majesty wishes me to repeat that as to Pond's Cream, it gives her daily greater satisfaction." A coupon was attached, bidding the reader to send for free sample tubes: "Send in the coupon today. The Queen of Roumania's loveliness may also be yours." To paint the lily, the company also asserted that the creams were "highly praised by Her Majesty, the Queen of Spain; the Duchesse De

Gramont; the Princesse Marie De Bourbon; Mrs. Nicholas Long-
worth, Mrs. Reginald Vanderbilt, and Miss Anne Morgan."

Europe imbued cachet. Elizabeth Hubbard, one of the early
successes in the skin-care field, set up a business in New York
that specialized in "Grecian preparations"; they had, as it turned
out, nothing at all to do with Greece. The already-legendary
Madame Helena Rubinstein told the story of her preparation, her
"finger of fate . . . my mother's beauty cream, first introduced to
my mother by a visiting actress friend, Modjeska. The cream was
made for her by a Hungarian chemist, Dr. Jacob Lykusky, then
living in Cracow . . . Mother encouraged all her daughters to use
it. 'It will make you beautiful,' she would whisper, kissing us
good night, 'And to be beautiful is to be a woman.' "

The most byzantine of all the stories accompanied the astringent Ambrosia, produced by a company founded by a woman
named Mrs. Hinze. Mrs. Hinze claimed that her formulation
dated back to the Second Empire; there it was conceived and born
by Mrs. Hinze's father and his chemist friend, André Verbillion.
Her father and Verbillion, she added, "played the clarinet side by
side during the Franco-Prussian War." Mrs. Hinze, like many of
the women who marketed their wares, would claim that she had
no intention of making the product available to the public—the
idea of a woman aspiring to make a buck was not considered
attractive then—but the overwhelming demand for Ambrosia's
healing powers compelled her to forsake her ladylike avocation
for the greater good. (Ambrosia, it turned out, which contained
carbolic acid, was roundly criticized by the New Hampshire
Board of Health, and it was taken off the market tout de suite.)

Estée would eventually spin out a lollapalooza of a yarn explaining her introduction to skin-care products to the *Palm Beach
Daily News* in April of 1965. The paper reported:

Back in 1939, when the first New York World's Fair began, Estee (you
pronounce it Estay, with the accent on the second syllable) was living
with her parents in Long Island, N.Y.

"An uncle of mine," she said, "who was a very famous skin specialist in Vienna came to New York because of the World's Fair . . . Then the war broke out and he couldn't go home. So he took a stable—it was an elegant stable—lined it with linoleum and began making skin creams there. I used to help him every chance I had. My family was always asking me, 'Why do you do it?' But I enjoyed it. Some of the creams I'd give to my friends. I gave the products away for years for nothing. In fact, I never changed doing that until we went into business."

The uncle to whom Estée made reference was, in the first place, not from Vienna but from a small Hungarian town named Miskolc in the north of Hungary. He was a younger brother of Estée's mother, and he was firmly ensconced in a modest chemical laboratory over the Longacre Theatre on Broadway when the World's Fair—on behalf of which some of the worst swamps in Corona were dredged—opened.

He was not a dermatologist but a chemist. He may or may not have had a Ph.D., but he was called Dr. Schotz. He was a good man. He made some good products. But he was, unfortunately, frightful when it came to business.

He arrived from Hungary in 1900. His citizenship papers describe Schotz as being five feet eight-and-a-half inches tall and having blue eyes, a Roman nose, brown hair, a fair complexion, and a long face. When Estée, his niece, was attending Newtown High School in Queens, he was living in a small house on Ocean Parkway in Brooklyn with his wife Flora Anna and her mother, a Mrs. Greenstein.

His business, New Way Laboratories, was established in 1924. His New Way Laboratories letterhead was a busy document that proclaimed "Special Attention to Private Formulas"; "Manufacturers of Wonderful Facial and Pigeon Remedy"; "We Make Up All Creams, Powders, Toilet Preparations and Mud Packs Under Your Own Name."

He compounded several beauty products: a Six-in-One Cold Cream, Dr. Schotz Viennese Cream, and several simple fragrances. He also made a poultry lice killer ("hold fowl by feet, head down . . . retail according to cost of making"), suppositories, Dog Mange Cure, lip rouge in a pot, muscle-building cream, paint and varnish remover, embalming fluid, painkillers, freckle remover, toothache drops, and Hungarian Mustache Wax.

Eventually Estée would work with John Schotz, peddling his beauty products, learning from him the technique of hands-on facial massage, which he practiced on the premises and which skill she used over the many lean years. How early she came to Uncle John is not determinable. He was, no gainsaying, her mentor; his products were responsible for her first success.

She was sixteen and calling herself Estelle when he set up his first business. She had attained her full height of five feet four-and-a-half inches, and according to family memories she was a very lovely young woman. Lucille Carlan Rottkov was related to John through his wife, Anna. Lucille is now a physician's wife, living in Fleischmanns, New York. She recalls that her mother, Olga, used to say, "Uncle John's niece Estelle is *so* beautiful." Estée had dark hazel eyes and a complexion that survived the Valley of the Ashes: It was pure and flawless and radiant. People remember that she had a most extraordinary complexion.

The 1925 New York State Census places Estée, as of June 1, 1925, at home over the hardware store at 172 Corona Avenue. She is called "Estella Mentzer"; Family Status: Daughter; Age: 16; Occupation: High School. Her sister, Grace, at eighteen, is still also in high school. Max Mentzer, Head of Household, Hardware Dealer, gives his age as forty-eight, out of obvious deference to his wife, Rose, housewife, who gives her true age, which was forty-nine.

According to the 1925 New York census, Estée at sixteen was a student in a New York high school, presumably Newtown High. Whether or not Estée graduated from there is unclear. Two theories exist as to what she did at this junction. One has her working with and around John Schotz; a second places her in Milwaukee, Wisconsin.

The second version is posited by Florian W. Harvat, who was then a beautician in the Milwaukee area; he was later to run a cosmetology school and was president for a time of the National Hairdressers and Cosmetologists Association. Harvat contends that he knew Estée through a friend named Catharine Zosobucki, who owned a beauty salon on the East Side of Milwaukee near Prospect Avenue, which was frequented by some prominent wives of the local brewers, including the Millers and Mrs. Uhline of the Schlitz family. Harvat contends that Estée was continuing her high school education there, living with her aunt Sarah, and working after school, with a girlfriend, who was presumably not Eve Harrington. Estée, he says, "was a little clean-up girl. She washed combs and brushes after school."

She was known as Estelle Mentzer, and Catharine, who has recently died, called her "the little snot." She stayed on or later returned to the Milwaukee area, selling her Uncle John's products up and down, from Milwaukee into Chicago. Harvat says, "Since she was known as Estelle Mentzer, a lot of those who might remember Estelle do not connect her with Estée Lauder."

Estée and Catharine, Harvat says, kept up a correspondence for years, Catharine chiding her ex-employee for selling out to the class market.

Edna L. Emme, president d'honneur of the National Hairdressers and Cosmetologists Association, agrees with Harvat's recollections: "Estée Lauder started in the beauty business in Milwaukee," Mrs. Emme says. "Originally, they all come into the beauty salons because the beauty salons are a good place to sell their products."

The plot thins. And Estée has been no help over the years. She would no more admit to washing combs and brushes on the East Side of Milwaukee than she would fess up to being raised over a hardware store that has become an Italian restaurant that displays pictures of Joe DiMaggio, Frank Sinatra, and the Pope, not to mention a lovely European lighting fixture that once belonged to Rose Mentzer.

The one certain thing is that Estée presently made a choice that turned out to be wise: She continued her involvement with the formulas of John Schotz, which were saved by his niece Lucille.

In 1985 a Revlon chemist commented on the Schotz skin-care formulas: "They're obviously very old-fashioned, but probably they were very efficacious. They lubricate. They're heavy. And they're probably very good still, if you have very dry skin. They wouldn't be as nice aesthetically as what you can buy today. But they're quite good for their time. The one containing methyl salicylate even contained a sunscreen. Whether Schotz recognized that or not, one doesn't know."

And Dr. Albert M. Kligman, professor of dermatology at the University of Pennsylvania School of Medicine, said of Schotz's "Florana Six-in-One": "That would work. Not very aesthetic. But functional, reliable, safe. Patentable? Certainly not."

Estée would soon make another choice that turned out to be functional, reliable, and ultimately safe. His name was Joseph Lauter—with a *t*. And he had a background very much like hers, though he never appeared to want to disavow it, except for Estée's sake. Joseph was born six years before Estée, on December 26, 1902. After a time, however, he would celebrate his birthday on Christmas day.

He was a sweet-looking, curly-haired young man. His parents, Lillian and William Lauter, were immigrants from Galicia, a section of Austria that was hardscrabble and much less hospitable to its Jews than bounteous Hungary. A successful immigrant merchant named Louis Bougenicht wrote in his autobiography: "To us in Galicia, Hungary was a golden land . . . In Hungary, we Galicians knew, people were modern, less bigoted, richer in the world's goods." Joe's parents had emigrated to the United States in the 1890s; his father, like Estée's, was a custom tailor. Joe was a middle son, born on the Lower East Side; he studied at the High School of Commerce, taking a course in shorthand. (His younger brother Herman became a legal stenographer.) He also studied accounting.

Estée recounts that they met near Mohegan, where Rose and Max had a summer home. Estée claimed he was playing golf at Rock Hill Lodge. Joe, she said, was smitten by the first sight of her in shorts and socks, and smitten he must have been. Though Estée's features were fine and her complexion radiant (some of the younger girls in the Lake Mohegan area looked upon her when she came to visit, in pearls and a city dress, as "a goddess"), her legs were never her strong or long suit. Apropos Estée's version of the meeting, *Women's Wear Daily* reported in 1985: "She confides he was looking at her for a long time before a friend introduced them and he said hello: 'I didn't say hello to him because I didn't talk to too many young men and my father was very strict.' " In an earlier *WWD* story, she had him calling her, "Hey, Blondie."

Estée was about nineteen when they met; Joe was twenty-five. They went together for three years. Joe was in and out of a series of failed businesses, with various partners. One was called Apex Silks; it was hit by the general sluggishness of the industry. Joe also sold buttons for a time. He was in a short-lived textile venture with yet another partner, whose relative remembers Joe and Estée as a couple: "She was very aloof when I met her: attractive, well dressed. He was good-looking and not too smart."

His partner's wife at Apex remembers her as Esther: "Esther, during their courtship, was living in Corona with her mother and father and lots of brothers. . . . She spent time at her uncle's place at Forty-second Street, but I don't really know what she did there. We socialized. I had a bridge game and a Mah-Jongg game, and a group of us met at Schrafft's. And she used to walk in and the topic would immediately come around to beautiful complexions. She had a gorgeous, gorgeous complexion."

Estée and Joe married on January 15, 1930, in the wake of the stock market crash. The ceremony took place at the Royal Palm at 135th Street and Broadway. He gave his occupation as "silk"; she listed no occupation. Their best man was Martin Adolf of 159 Ross Street, Brooklyn; their witnesses were Ethel Grosshandler and Irma Weiner.

The years that followed the marriage are sparsely chronicled. When Estée was asked about them, she replied with amorphous references to hard work and more of it. She would eventually whine that no one believed in her, among them the famous Chicago-based cosmetics entrepreneur Dorothy Gray. She even once made the extraordinary remark, "No one taught me—usually girls have a father or an uncle to help them. But people said to me, 'You'll never get ahead in New York City, you'll never get any further.' "

She did say that she started her business during the Depression; that there was no such thing as bad business, only bad business people: "Women will open their purses for quality." It is safe to assume that she began during this time to sell her uncle's creams avocationally. There are references to beach clubs and Hadassah lunches and other charity functions where she sold the creams and gave them as gifts, with full faith that the quality of her merchandise would be appreciated and the women would come back for more.

With Estée's energy as a given, it is impossible to assume that she stayed home idle while Joe went out into the marketplace. In 1932 they were in at least one commercial venture together, reported by Marilyn Bender to have been a cafeteria. The assertion is buttressed by the fact that she and Joe—Estelle Lauter and

Joseph Lauter—were plaintiffs in an action against C & L Lunch Co., Inc., a corporation that included two sandwich shops on upper Broadway.

Their first child, Leonard Allan Lauter, was born in New York City on March 19, 1933, that same year a listing appeared in the Manhattan telephone directory for Lauter Associates Chemists.

Estée's first appearance in the New York telephone directory as "Estee Lauder" was in the summer of 1937, at 173 West Seventy-eighth Street; Joseph, at the same address, had yet to change his name from Lauter to Lauder. By 1938 Estelle Lauder is in Greenwich Village; Joe is nowhere in the Manhattan pages.

She divorced Joe on grounds of mental cruelty in Miami Beach, Florida, on April 11, 1939. Presumably Joe wasn't taking her where she wanted to go, which was up.

Aida DeMaris, a neighbor of Estée's, who belonged to the Atlantic Beach Club and dressed with her there, remembers Estée as "a very attractive, very ambitious young woman . . . I know she was very ambitious, very anxious to get on with the thing."

There was the boast of privilege, and stables, and choosing to work; there was the whine of fathers and uncles who were no help at all. And she must have seen Joe as just such a helpless mate.

She took the boy Leonard and went out to find a man with power.

3

SEPARATION

During her three-year separation from Joe, from 1939 until 1942, Estée traveled back and forth between New York City and Miami Beach, where she set up a concession at the swank Roney Plaza Hotel on Collins Avenue. Her Uncle John suggested that she go to Miami and attempt to sell his skin creams there. It was around this time that she met one of the men on whom she apparently set her sights, Dr. John Myers, an Englishman who earned a degree in dentistry and then made a substantial amount of money in oil and flanges; he was also a philanthropist who had organized a foundation to aid young and promising artists. Myers was eighteen years older than Estée. Lucille Carlan Rottkov, John Schotz's niece, contends that Myers was helpful to Estée financially. He would eventually marry actress Tina Louise's stepmother in the mid-forties and became involved in a highly publicized, slightly messy divorce.

Myers's daughter from a previous marriage, Jeannette M. Vitkin, who is president of the Myers Foundation and was eighteen at the time, recalls accompanying Myers and Estée when they went out dining and dancing. Mrs. Vitkin had no idea of Estée's involvement in cosmetics and was annoyed when Estée, rather nervily she thought, suggested, "You shouldn't wear that lipstick. It's not right for you."

Estée's boldness was more and more manifest. She frequently stopped perfect strangers on the street, suggesting makeup changes to them, sometimes walking away with a forty-dollar sale of her products. Once she stopped a Salvation Army sister and told her that her calling was no excuse for personal dowdiness. Somehow or other she was developing the force and the charisma to pull such oddities off without offending or getting herself into unseemly situations or temporary restraints.

Estée lived in New York at a couple of addresses up and down the West Seventies on or near West End Avenue. One neighbor of hers recalls that Estée's relationship with the man in Florida did not work out, and another that she "was trying very hard to stand on her own two feet." Mrs. Rose Schapiro lived on "the seventh or eighth floor" of Estée's West End Avenue building; Mrs. Schapiro was paying $106 a month for a four-room apartment and assumes Estée was paying about $125 for one slightly larger: "She was businesslike, always in a hurry. I'd see her in the elevator with her son, who was maybe six at the time."

According to the wife of one of Joe's ex-business partners, young Leonard, who was "crazy about his father . . . was having trouble with his speech. . . . Estée took him to a special school, and, for the most part, he got over it." The same woman remembers Leonard as "a grand boy." Joe was around and about—at some point he took up residence at the Paris Hotel on upper West End Avenue, and he was courting Estée "like nobody's business." He wanted Blondie back.

Estée continued to travel to the various resort areas: Grossinger's in the Catskill Mountains and the Lido Beach Club. She gave facials free, hoping to impress her customers enough to have them back as future buyers, and it often worked. She hawked her products right on the beach at another club in Nassau County, where she also had a cabana. Her clientele were mostly middle- to upper-middle-class Jewish women, with whom Estée apparently had an incredible rapport.

She met another man during this period who had a major

impact on her career in fragrance. Some believe she lived with him, although he was married at the time. He was a Dutch-born industrialist, Arnold Lewis van Ameringen. He was a legend even then in his field. And through a series of mergers, he would become president and chairman of the board of International Flavors & Fragrances, Inc., the largest creator of fragrances and flavorings in the United States; in addition to making most of the major fragrances in the world, the company flavors and creates the odor for many of the products on the American market.

He was sixteen years older than Estée, an amateur magician, a high-stakes card player. He became intensely interested in mental health and the usefulness of fragrance and cosmetics to combat despondency; he founded and funded Fountain House, one of the first halfway houses for psychiatric outpatients in the country. He has been described as "an industrialist of the old school, a real gentlemen who looked like something out of Condé Nast, pince-nez and all."

Much of his funding came from fragrance giant Pierre Wertheimer, the president of Chanel. A man who handled the Chanel fragrances in Europe remembers hearing about Estée for the first time through Wertheimer. Wertheimer called her van Ameringen's "girlfriend" and predicted that she'd go far.

A distinguished heir to a department store fortune comments, "She had a boyfriend when she got the divorce from Joe; he became the head of I.F.F." A society press agent contends that she was told of the relationship by a close relative of van Ameringen's.

They broke apart finally, some say because he would not leave his wife, Hedwig, whom he had married soon after his arrival in the United States in 1917 and to whom he would remain married for life. They had three children, one of whom is now vice-president of I.F.F. in Paris.

One of Estée's West End Avenue women friends—many of whom are still living in their large, rent-controlled apart-ments—summed up, "She thought she'd go out on her own and meet all kinds of millionaires. That doesn't happen so fast. And she was getting fed up with the kind of people she was meeting. Different men. You know, people don't just hand things over. And so she said to me, 'What am I knocking myself out for with other guys? Joe's a nice man. I don't know why I broke off with him.' And she decided to go back and make it a family thing and bring him into the business and accomplish things."

Estée remarried Joe, who had never given up on her, on December 7, 1942. He listed his profession as "salesman"; she, stubbornly, as "housewife." She was at 305 West End Ave; he at 752 West End Avenue. He moved into her apartment. He was thirty-nine; she had become, by this time, thirty-one, giving her birth date as July 1, 1911. One of their witnesses was Estée's sister, Mrs. Renée Shapiro of Jackson Heights, Queens, and one Thelma Ellis of 1049 Park Avenue. Renée had married a businessman named Herman Shapiro in 1926, at the Château de Luxe in the Bronx.

Estée was determined to bring Joe into her business. He became, at some later point, a trustee of the Brooklyn College School of Pharmacy, and it is possible that he studied there for a time to prepare himself for his mid-life career change. One former neighbor recounts, "She told me that she was going back with him and she was *really* going to put her shoulder to the wheel and *really* get into the business seriously. And she did. And she got her husband into it."

The product of their reunion and their last child was Ronald S. Lauder, born February 26, 1944. Estée set up her first office at 39 East Sixtieth Street.

She was all over the place; Joe minded the store and watched the children. According to a woman who has been very close to Estée Lauder through the years, and is herself a legend in the cosmetics field, Estée worked behind counters: "She had to. I taught her. When she started, I said, 'You don't know a *thing* about the girl behind the counter. You get back there and learn.'

28

Nobody can become a cosmetician unless they stand in back of the counter. She stood there in stocking feet and she sold. She was at Bonwit Teller; she was all over the country. Just her own line, nobody else's. She was a good salesgirl."

Sara Fredericks, who owns several exclusive dress shops in Palm Beach, New York, and Boston remembers, "In the old days, she was behind the counter, and she had a marvelous rapport, if you know what I mean, with the powers in the store."

Estée worked in and eventually oversaw a few tiny concessions in beauty salons, selling her line, which had come to include about six products: her uncle's wondrous Creme Pack, his All-Purpose Creme, and his cleansing oil. There were also some products that she might have purchased from independent manufacturers: a lipstick called Just Red, a face powder, and a turquoise eye shadow. Irma Shorell, who remembers Estée as beautiful and savvy, worked under her for a time and then took over at the Florence Morris beauty salon when Estée went out to begin other similar concessions in Manhattan and Brooklyn.

The Florence Morris space was a tiny, raised area; Estée stood behind a counter with her products and mixed well with the women who frequented the salon. Back then, women were compelled to spend a good deal of time sitting under hot dryers, with nothing but free time and melting makeup.

One customer of Florence Morris remembers Estée approaching her one day as she sat under a dryer. Estée suggested that the woman try her creams; she applied the product to her face and hands. ("Touch your customer and you're halfway there," she would teach her own acolytes.) The woman, who was pregnant at the time, still regards Estée fondly. She remembers her dazzling smile and her great warmth. She told Estée about the pregnancy. When her baby was born, she received a big basket of Estée's products.

Estée worked at a shop run by a Mrs. Wyler, a big, blond woman who threw towels over her mirrors so that her customers

29

could not watch as she cut their hair. A writer named Helen Baum was there: "Estée had a tiny, tiny corner and she stood behind it selling the creams that she was probably making in her bathroom."

Estée did finally convince Bonwit Teller on Fifth Avenue to take her products; and she spent her Saturdays there, all day, on her feet, selling her wares. But her dream was to be in Saks Fifth Avenue. It was considered the most elegant department store in New York; only Saks and Macy's devoted any considerable space (which was and is called real estate in the trade) to the sale of cosmetics. And according to Bob Fiske, who was the cosmetics buyer at Saks at the time, "If you weren't in Saks, you weren't in business."

Fiske knew that Estée was in Bonwit's, that "she was quite a huckster," and that her line did moderately well there. But he found no need to introduce the Estée Lauder line into Saks. In the first place, it was in Bonwit's; and Saks insisted on exclusivity. Additionally, the Saks customers had demonstrated no particular desire to have the Lauder line in the store. The management at Saks attempted to cater to and satisfy the demands of their customers. If a customer requested a product that Saks did not carry, a Saks employee would actually go out and purchase it at retail and sell it at the same price. If sufficient demand was expressed for a particular product, Saks considered carrying it.

There were buying hours at the Saks offices every Wednesday and Friday afternoons. During these hours, Estée sat, along with forty or fifty other merchants, all avid to be placed in Saks, outside Fiske's office. She explained to Fiske repeatedly that his customers wanted and needed her line; he countered that no such desire was showing up in their experience. He finally told her, "In the absence of that demand, we're not going to give any further consideration to your product."

Estée replied, "I'm going to prove to you that Saks customers want my product."

"If that's so," Fiske said, "we'll give consideration to it."

At the time, Estée was involved with some kind of lecturing or demonstration program, and she worked the women's charity-luncheon circuit. She was scheduled to speak at a benefit luncheon at the Starlight Roof of the Waldorf-Astoria Hotel. Fiske insists that Estée was speaking about something other than cosmetics and that her spiel came after the lecture. That assertion seems unlikely to those who know Estée and who contend that her sentences, when they are not directly related to her products, seldom include more than three or four words. In any case, Estée told Fiske that she would demonstrate the demand for her product at the Waldorf. Fiske dispatched a representative to monitor Estée's performance.

Estée would tell a modified version of what was probably the selfsame episode to Marilyn Bender of *The New York Times*. This is how Bender reported Estée's account: " 'I gave my stock out of charity, and God has been good to me because of that,' she said. She referred to a benefit luncheon at the Starlight Roof of the Waldorf-Astoria. 'I gave them a $3.00 lipstick. It was a time during the war when you couldn't get metal cases. They said, "Why don't you give plastic?" When I give anything, I give something. I had forty calls after that asking couldn't I do the same for them and I said yes. I feel God has repaid me,' she said, raising her right hand, 'if you give, you get.' "

Whichever version is the more accurate, Estée *got* as a result of that charity luncheon at the Waldorf. Fiske recalls, "As the luncheon broke up, there formed a line of people across Park Avenue and across Fiftieth Street into Saks asking for these lipsticks, one after another. It convinced us that there was a demand for the Lauder product." Estée got her space at Saks, and that space imbued her product with the cachet that made it that much easier to sell nationally.

And around the country she went. Throughout the following decade, from the mid-forties through the mid-fifties, she traveled to specialty and department stores, hawking the Estée Lauder line. She made personal appearances. She trained sales help on proper selling techniques. She rewarded important buyers with promises, promises, and expensive dinners. To two very eminent, important women buyers, she promised stock in her company when it went public; they are both quick to point out that (a) Estée's company never went public and (b) it was the woman, her energy, her incredible pitching talents that impressed them and not her promises.

Joe worked from 8:00 A.M. to 7:00 P.M. seven days a week. Leonard pitched in whenever he could, helping in the small space they had rented to make the products, delivering the goods to Saks on his bicycle on weekends and before school. He remembers that once during his adolescence his mother was away for twenty-five weeks.

He also remembers being at a meeting after Estée and Joe decided to invest seriously in the business. There is a piece of paper that signifies that Estée Lauder formed a company in 1947 (Joe's name was not yet on the document); that was probably the year of the meeting. Their accountant-lawyer, in the presence of fourteen-year-old Leonard who was practically a member of the firm, told Estée and Joe that investing seriously in the cosmetics business, with its high mortality rate, was ill advised, insane.

They disregarded his advice, and with good reason, over and above the incredible faith Estée had in herself and her abilities. The postwar business of beauty was booming. An article in *The New York Times Magazine* of May 12, 1946, begins: "Beauty is a billion-dollar business. By the end of 1946, the American woman will have spent, within the year, $700,000,000 on cosmetics. Because of her the drug store on Main Street, the Fifth Avenue department store, the five-and-ten, and even the food chains sell powder, paint and perfume . . . Among 50,000,000 American women, the glamour market is solid. It was found in a recent sampling of 1,000 women that 99 percent used lipstick, 95 percent nail polish, 94 percent face powder, 80 percent makeup base, 73 percent perfume, and 71 percent cleansing cream."

Obviously, the industry was outgrowing, or growing beyond, the skin-care products that John Schotz was now manufacturing with some semimanual equipment in his laboratory on West Seventy-second Street. However, Estée was continuing to sell several of his products: the six-in-one cream, the cold cream, and doubtless other of his products. Estée would boast that it was "Schatz's" creams (she never did get the spelling of his last name or his nativity right) that cleared up a scar on playwright Vicki Baum's skin and also helped some skin problems Saks buyer Marion Coombs was experiencing.

There is a difference of opinion as to how it was that Estée grew rich while Schotz stayed poor. He and his sweet wife, Flora Anna Schotz, were never ahead of the game. They had suffered their worst days during the Depression, when they and her mother were thrown out of their house onto the street for failure to make payments on the property. Lucille Rottkov, whose mother Olga took them in, remembers, "I'll never forget seeing my grand-mother and my Uncle John and Anna on the street on Ocean Parkway with their mattress and their bedspread."

Lucille contends further that Uncle John was not paid "five cents" by his niece for the skin-care products. If he grew fat along with her, it was surely not reflected in his life-style, his habitat, or his estate. He and Anna rented a one-bedroom apartment on West Seventy-second Street and owned a rundown lot in Hunt-ington, New York, with chicken coops, pigeons, and an assort-ment of visiting children. They never had any children of their own, and they took in one nephew, an orphan, and several other youngsters temporarily—all of whom loved being around them.

Lucille Rottkov's younger brother, Alan Carlan, who is now in the aerospace industry in California, remembers being in John's laboratory and alongside his uncle feeding the pigeons in Hunt-ington. He remembers seeing letters of appreciation and commendation on John's office walls: one from Vicki Baum, one from the wife of Premier Clemenceau of France. He remembers, too, that his uncle said to him, "I gave her the formulas." He does not know whether or not he was remunerated.

Schotz died barely solvent, leaving Anna nothing because he had been compelled to cash in his life insurance. By that time, in the sixties, Estée was not a living legend, but she *was* succeeding. She took his widow Anna out to lunch and showed her her new plant on Long Island. When Anna died, alone on West Seventy-second Street, a few years after, Estée was contacted by Lucille. Estée advised her to "look under the beds and behind the bathtub. You know how Hungarians are. They hide things."

Even now Lucille has other problems with Estée. Aside from harboring resentment about John's and Anna's poverty, she bristles: "Why did she have to say he was Viennese in *Vogue*?" She would also like to ask Estée to pay for the perpetual care on Uncle John's grave. But she hasn't mustered the resolution yet to do that.

4

YOUTH-DEW

As with so many features of her developing company, the phenomenon in the cosmetics business—which came to be known as gift-with-purchase—was not only efficacious, but was also a function and a facet of Estée's developing personality. She believed evangelically in the superiority of everything she sold, and by reaching out a gift hand she was promising, "Try it. I know you'll like it. I *know* you'll want more."

A buyer who worked around her when she opened her Neiman-Marcus account compares Estée to several other women with whom he has dealt over the years: Martha, the Palm Beach and Park Avenue couturière; Mildred Custin, the department-store executive; and Mary Kay, the mesmeric mass-market cosmetics queen who recently bought back the company that was not working as a public corporation. "They don't talk to you," he says, "they *preach* to you. They're such believers in what they're doing. All they talk about is their product."

Of course, that kind of apostolic ardor can be attributed to men as well. But it was that much more a necessary and vitalizing attribute of the successful woman, who in most cases could *only* rise to the top if she created the company in the first place, and even then she was compelled to point out the uncle or the chemist or the clarinet player who was responsible for the formula. These Furies never had a Gaea in their family tree.

What aided and abetted Estée's rise was the extraordinary and *creative* vigor with which she used gift-with-purchase and the giving away of samples. She and Joe had no choice but to sample. When they had amassed fifty or sixty thousand dollars, which was probably by the late forties, they went out shopping for an advertising agency. Someone suggested BBD&O, whose resident genius then was a man named Ben Duffy, whom we may assume Estée would have chosen to see. He was handling Campbell's Soup, Lever Brothers, Lucky Strike, and Revlon. The Lauders were told, quite simply, that fifty thousand dollars wasn't nearly enough capital to finance an effective advertising campaign.

They chose a more direct route to their potential customers. The money was used to make up samples and to print mailers letting their potential customers know that a gift awaited them at whatever store they were then peddling their line of skin-care products. At Saks Fifth Avenue, Estée had the help and enthusiastic admiration of a young man named Bob Wirtz, who was the direct-mail manager there. "She got involved in direct mail and what we call cycle-billing," Wirtz recalled. "Those are the bill inserts that the customers receive every month. We did a tremendous amount of direct mail for Estée in the early fifties."

The Saks mailing list was pure gold. And Estée apparently had the ability to induce people to want to help her. Wirtz might even have been a bit smitten with her. He recalls, "She was a magnificent-looking woman . . . I just loved her as a personality. And she was a man's woman in a man's world. And you cannot believe how feminine she remained: She could cope with the domineering male presence with which she was confronted day in and day out. She had a flair for making people like her."

And believe in her. Agnes Ash, who would become editor of the *Palm Beach Daily News*, remembers seeing Estée for the first time when Agnes walked into what she calls "a low-end store that might have been Ohrbach's in New York" in 1950. She compared Estée's personality to Madame Helena Rubinstein's: "They both established quick rapport . . . I remember going and seeing Estée, and we had a discussion about some herbal cream. And I just knew that it was going to do me some good. And indeed it did. She took it very seriously and she was convincing. I really felt that she was interested; that it was not just a big, mass-produced *thing*."

Estée continued to traipse around the country in the early fifties. She opened up accounts and trained line women, saving every possible penny to sock back into the business. She had someone who put her up in Florida; she ate at company cafeterias, thrilled to save money on lunch; she schlepped her line on trains and buses. If Estée Lauder was on the map it was because Estée Lauder was all over the map.

Harry Doyle, a young salesman on the road for Revlon at the time, remembers meeting her in 1950 or 1951. She was about to launch her line in Neiman-Marcus' Dallas store. (Neiman's head man, Stanley Marcus, would write in later years of encountering the young Estée Lauder "who came in swinging like Sugar Ray Robinson.") Doyle was in San Antonio at a store whose cosmetic buyer, Edna Darwin, asked, "Would you drive Estée Lauder to Dallas?" Harry replied, "Who the hell is Estée Lauder?"

Edna Darwin explained, "She's got a treatment line and she has to get back to Dallas to give a class there."

Harry drove Estée, who was going to instruct a group of Neiman women about the care and handling of her products and then take them all out to dinner. He took her back to the Adolphus Hotel, where she changed her clothes in time for the 6:30 class. She talked during the forty-mile ride about her products and the expectations she had for the line at Neiman-Marcus.

He met her the following week at a store called Frost Brothers, and the week after that in Houston. Harry, to this day, has great admiration for Estée Lauder, remembering, "It's *hot* in Texas in June. And by her bootstraps is how she was doing it. Indomitable spirit, Estée!"

Estée schlepped. Estée hawked. Estée instructed. Estée cultivated: anyone who could help her professionally or socially. She got her products into I. Magnin in San Francisco because the chief buyer there, Van Venneri, a beautiful young woman of Calabrian extraction who was born in Walla Walla, liked Estée, liked the products, and liked the idea that it was a woman who was out doing it. Magnin is what is referred to in the trade as a "passport store"; if you were in Magnin you were given a certain credence and respect by other retailers. Magnin had Estée's products exclusively in the San Francisco area until the late seventies.

Estée's "best friend" in the Chicago area was Gladys Hyman, who introduced her to the buyer at Marshall Field; and among Estée's first important accounts was Marshall Field on State Street. Buyers in general were well disposed to Estée.

But not everyone either liked or approved of her. Having targeted the class stores as the only proper marketplace for her product, Estée early on decided to "avoid" being Jewish. A friend who helped Estée considerably when Estée was just starting out contends, "For *years* she wouldn't admit that she was Jewish. She disgraced herself . . . There was a buyer named Sally Freed who worked at Bergdorf who told Estée, 'You should be ashamed *not* to admit you're a Jew.' "

While Estée continued to travel, Joe was minding the store, which by now included two small plants in upper Manhattan. He was doing most of what is called "the bulk work"—filling the jars, often with the help of young Leonard. Leonard was just graduating from the Bronx High School of Science (which Estée conveniently managed to call the High School of Science, omitting any reference to the outer borough) and apparently was savvy enough for his parents to consider leaving him in charge of the plant operation while they took a vacation. He got chicken pox, thus ending the planned vacation and the trial run of the young Lauder.

Leonard was about to go off to attend the Wharton School at the University of Pennsylvania, where he would study business and prepare to enter the family firm. His account of how he spent his adolescence would differ considerably from the historical family portrait Estée usually paints. In 1985 he would tell a group of professional women: "As a child, I wasn't rich. Others had cars and summer houses in East Hampton. I worked as a waiter in a summer camp and then as a counselor. I dreamed of owning and someday running a company of my own."

Ronald, who graduated from the Bronx High School of Science a decade later, could have had no such recollections of not being rich. There had been a turning point in the intervening years: a phenomenon which brought Estée incredible and rather sudden ascendance to fame (within the industry) and fortune (or at least a pretty good leap into affluence). It was the creation of her first fragrance. It was a bath oil called Youth-Dew. It had the impact of a brass section and the perdurability of Methuselah. And American women took to it zealously.

For some time Estée had had fragrance on her mind. It was the obvious next step in the development of her business. Arden and Rubinstein had both begun in skin care and then developed fragrances. Estée's Youth-Dew not only captured the imagination of the American public, it practically made them stand up and cheer. But its genesis was unclear. Earlier, of course, she had worked with the fragrant products of her Uncle John.

John's formulas for cold cream included, for instance, the simple directions: "Apply heat again and stir until snow white and add oil of rose and pour into jars." Estée fooled around on that level when she went back to visit the Leppel sisters in the old neighborhood just as she was starting out in business. The store was now selling notions, including a ten-cent face cream. Estée did something to it, and the sisters marveled, "You'd never know it was the Pond's."

But that was a street song compared to the incredible symphony that is a modern, professional fragrance, the development of which requires vast expenditures, great peril, and a rare mixture of art, chemistry, and imagination that is the arcane precinct of the perfumer.

With the development of a fragrance in mind, Estée went to consult with her old friend, A. L. van Ameringen. He was then president of van Ameringen-Haebler, Inc., which subsequently merged with another company to become International Flavors and Fragrances. Even then, in the early fifties, A. L. van Ameringen, whose friends called him Van, was a giant in the field, and his company was the biggest in the business. How he helped is a matter of some question; *that* he helped is beyond doubt.

The man who is said to have developed Youth-Dew for Estée at I.F.F., Ernest Shiftan, who was called "Mr. Nose, USA," once said that "a good perfumer has to have an odor memory of 3,000 aromatic chemicals and natural resources . . . blend as many as 300 . . . consider lastingness, strength, evenness—beauty."

Writing about the ingredients of a typical fragrance—not Youth-Dew but one equally complex—the *Reader's Digest* in 1961 reported: "A single ounce of a currently favorite brand contains the essence of 9,600 jasmine flowers from France (at $700 a pound for jasmine absolute); 480 roses from France; 80 roses of a different variety from Morocco, 1,750 orange blossoms, 60 tuberoses . . . peel of half a bergamot from Calabria . . . handscraped peel of 15 oranges, sandalwood and cardamom oils from India; estragon oil from Spanish tarragon leaves; 3 animal fixatives (including a tincture from civet cat fed raw sheep in Ethiopia); 85 laboratory-made aromatic chemicals some of which go through 20 stages before purity is attained."

The perfumer trains for years to develop "a nose" and to keep alive in (usually) *his* head the memory of odors, so that he will know how they will blend. This he does with strange mnemonic tricks, one of them oddly related to geometry. Writing in *Drug & Cosmetic Industry* in February of 1958, J. R. Elliott recounted the experiences of the student perfumer: "As the student perfumer continues in his study of the various odors (both single and complex), he will gradually discover that with each odor stimulation his mind will form specific mental pictures or geometric figures . . . The student should not regard the bizarre shape and color in which these picture-forms often appear as mild mental aberrations, but rather a normal psychological experience."

What shape van Ameringen's help came in is subject to various interpretations. A man who was an important and extremely prestigious department store owner in the fifties asserts, "As far as I know, he *gave* her a present of Youth-Dew, which he thought would be a tremendous help in her business."

Robert Kramer, a past president of the Society of Cosmetic Chemists, asserts that Ameringen's company "really backed her heavily when she didn't have enough money to buy stuff. . . . They gave her credit when she needed it badly."

Don Davis, a cosmetics-industry editor, speculates, "He was in a position to do her a lot of good. He was even then the head of the biggest company in the business."

Eventually, of course, Estée would pay more than her way, becoming one of I.F.F.'s most loyal and most important customers. But, back then, she was an old friend going to a mogul for a favor—a favor that would turn her business around.

Introduced at Bonwit's in 1953 as a bath oil, Youth-Dew was something that you dumped in the tub and that adhered to the skin because of the high concentration of essential oils. It conformed to what was a market hungry for an assertive, tenacious, and unsubtle essence. Andy Lucarelli, who would go to work for Estée in the sixties, comments on the Youth-Dew success: "Youth-Dew was like the Giorgio of today. It just had that cachet. Middle America went bananas for it. . . . Every time she opened an account somewhere, they came out of the hills for it. . . . The fragrance had a lot of punch. It was long-lasting. She gave the American woman a bath oil that substituted for a perfume. They could buy it for $8.50 and have a perfume that lasted for twenty-four hours. It was a whole new direction, and it was affordable. Middle America felt that it was getting its money's worth."

Estée used Youth-Dew in the beginning as a sampler, a try-it-you'll-like-it kind of thing. And they tried it, and they loved it, and they bought it. The success and drawing power of the fragrance redounded well to the rest of the Estée Lauder line. People were lured into buying her treatment products by the offer of a free sampling of Youth-Dew. Richard Salomon comments, "Until Youth-Dew arrived on the scene there wasn't anything for us at Charles of the Ritz to worry about. . . . Her treatment line wasn't big and it wasn't of consequence; even the packaging looked like it was put together with loving hands. But Youth-Dew hit. Right away. Lauder went from a volume of maybe three or four hundred a week in a store like Neiman-Marcus to maybe five thousand a week. Nobody did five thousand a week in those days. . . . The draw of Youth-Dew and a gift with purchase . . . It was very clever of her to use a fragrance item to promote the sale of treatment products, and it showed volume."

At Saks, Youth-Dew accounted for about 80 percent of her business by the mid-fifties. By that time, according to Bob Fiske, Estée was well on her way to becoming "a very dominant factor on the cosmetics scene. She had bypassed Dorothy Gray, who was probably the number-three treatment line. She was not yet up to Rubinstein or Arden, but she was growing."

Estée, of course, wore her new fragrance everywhere, and spritzed it on friends whether they liked it or not, and induced her widening circle of social friends to use it and talk about it. Designer Jo Copeland, who was a big name in fashion during this period, did everything possible to promote and proclaim the merits of the fragrance.

Estée did almost no print advertising for it. If one were an anosmic nonshopper, one could have missed the phenomenon entirely. But there was no missing it or its impact while in the stores themselves. Bob Fiske remembers that Saks was totally suffused with it. She sprayed it in the elevators; the entire area carried the message of Youth-Dew. "She did a superb job with it," Fiske says. "Nobody could escape the fragrance."

Once a woman from a rival house met Estée for lunch in a small Italian restaurant where the odor of Parmesan cheese usually reigned supreme. The fragrance-conscious woman smelled no cheese at all, only the odor of Estée's Youth-Dew, which the woman hated: "To me," she says, "it's always smelled like pure vanilla."

Nobody liked Youth-Dew but the customers. Savants called it vulgar, cloying, brassy, and nauseating.

"I hate it. It's vulgar. I wish I had a piece of it," Harry Doyle comments.

As a giveaway, as a gift-with-purchase, as a bath oil, and finally as a perfume, Youth-Dew, in its many variations, catapulted Estée's whole business: it made her a factor to be considered, if not yet a force to be reckoned with, in the business. It ushered in the amazing rebirth of gift-with-purchase. And it still makes $30 million a year worldwide.

And, by 1955, it permitted the Lauders—Estée, Joe, Leonard, and Ronald—to move out of 310 West End Avenue to their first town house at 13 East Seventy-seventh Street. Estée told *WWD* that this would give "the children . . . more room to play."

5

THE BEGINNING
OF THE BEGINNING

When Leonard Lauder officially joined Estée Lauder, Inc. in 1958 he was just out of the navy where he had served as a supply officer on an aircraft carrier. He was twenty-four, the spitting image of Joe, still stammering, and hardly sartorial. Estée was chagrined by the fact that Leonard still wore his blue navy-issue shoes and that a little bit of flesh showed every time he crossed his legs. She instructed Robert Nielson, executive vice-president, to take her son out and teach him how to dress.

Andy Lucarelli—young, creative, flamboyant—brought over from Saks to do a little bit of everything, including attempting to form a separate art department at Lauder, remembers how nervous and uptight Leonard was in those days, "Always on edge. He could be sincere and warm and good, yet terribly erratic."

Leonard called his mother "Mrs. Lauder" at work and in front of whatever press they managed to attract at the time—a sensible protocol they had obviously worked out. But over and above this formality, the Lauder staff discerned a closeness between Estée and Ronald, who was still in school but on view occasionally, that did not seem to exist between her and Leonard.

She made Leonard very nervous. Tony Liebler had been asked to join the company by Robert Nielson. Liebler had been with Pan Am and had never even heard of Estée. Liebler and Nielson were members of the same club. Liebler learned from Nielson and became sales manager of the New York area. He is now one of the top men at the knavish Paco Rabanne. Liebler observes, "I think Leonard had to *prove* to her that he was capable."

In his personal life, Leonard remained his own man. There was a time, for instance, when he dated a real live princess who lived down the road from Estée in Palm Beach. The prospect of a royal wedding, of course, thrilled Estée. But in 1959 Leonard married an elementary school teacher, Evelyn Hausner. Her parents, refugees from an Austria that had changed since Franz Josef, owned a hosiery store in Manhattan. She was dark, attractive, smart, and—*mirabile dictu*—Vienna-born. When she was pregnant with their first child, she chipped in at the company, answering the phone. She joked in later years about playing games then to create the impression that Lauder was more than two rooms and twelve people.

Leonard had reason to be nervous. He was being groomed to lead. He cared *intensely* about the success of a business that had been a ubiquitous part of his life since infancy. And to fail Estée Lauder, Inc. was to fail Estée Lauder: "She is the company, the company is she," he would assert.

In addition to his other responsibilities, Leonard was apparently compelled to keep the secrets, to disclose minimally. Later on that would become a more pervasive problem. When journalist Jean Baer, for instance, came to interview him for a book she was preparing on successful Jews, the self-chosen, she carried a list of questions prepared for her eyes only—a guide to areas of possible exploration.

Among her hastily typed questions: "Did you ever feel deprived because you had a working mother? How did you meet your wife? Where did your parents meet? Jewish upbringing?" After the usual formalities, Leonard asked to see her sheet of paper. He scanned the list, handed it back to her, and said matter-of-factly, "These are questions I would not answer."

Leonard seemed to have a very different attitude than Estée did about being Jewish. He stayed home on the High Holy Days and made no secret of his observance. Estée, on the other hand, was always conveniently "away." When Estée was on to bigger and better residences, Leonard had no problem using the little house at Lake Mohegan, where he and Evelyn were active in the temple. It became, somehow, Leonard's house, and he would commute during the summer by train, his head buried in company documents.

He had official, evanescent titles and owned one-third of the company, but it was clear to all who ran Estée Lauder, Inc. Once, when Estée was away, Leonard and the staff had prepared and made ready for production a new skin cream, which he finally presented to his mother at a meeting. She said to Leonard that she had no objection to the manufacture of this new product, "as long as you put your name on it and not mine."

While Lauder trekked toward its first million and Leonard bought socks, the research laboratories of France, which had always taken the care and "feeding" of the skin, as opposed to its embellishment, more seriously than their American counterparts, were turning out a spate of new, organically based substances claimed to enhance and protract the look of youth and to slough off the signs of aging.

The French cosmetic houses were researching and marketing products derived from hormones, serums, marine algae, and polyunsaturates, more intensively merging science with pricey merchandising techniques.

In August of 1960 there was a rather good and prophetic address made by a widely regarded merchandising and advertising expert named George J. Abrams, president of the Hudnut-DuBarry division of Warner-Lambert. He talked to his audience of specialty-store owners about the changes that were taking place in European skin care and bade them think about the proper marketplace for such products in the United States.

He called these preparations "charmaceuticals" and advised his audience to receive them appropriately: in specialty stores with a character of their own, where attention could be properly paid. What was in it for the merchandiser, he said, were more satisfied customers and larger profits, since the new products were more expensive than the general run of cosmetics. Furthermore, he said, though they could be presold to a point, the products needed explaining for proper use: "They [the products] plead for instruction. This gives you and the department stores a virtual exclusive on their sale."

European skin care was readily received in Europe. But in the United States, the Food and Drug Administration (FDA) tolerated far less than its European counterparts. The FDA, however, was cracking down on the promulgation of claims about certain miracle ingredients. DuBarry's Crème Natal and Queen Hélène's Gift of Life were confiscated, both part of the spate of placental creams that were coming into vogue in this country.

New products and their advertising claims began to sing the song of science. Helena Rubinstein did a "deep-pore" Bio-Facial Treatment. Revlon promised that its Ultima Cream penetrated "into the living cells." Elizabeth Arden produced Crème Extraordinaire, "protecting," "redirecting." Cosmétiques Biotherm incorporated "plankton, the tiny primal organisms in the living water of Earth."

Estée climbed aboard. But she was smarter than most. She called her new cream Re-Nutriv. And, typically, the thrust of the claim would be in the name, a name that said nothing and everything, and remained well outside the purview of the FDA. To this point, her skin-care products were quite reasonably priced. She had something called "Crème Plastique" for $5.00;

47

an eye cream to combat eye puffiness for $2.50 and $3.00; a "Super-Rich All-Purpose Crème," which cleaned and lubricated for $2.50 and $5.00; and a "Special Throat Crème" for: "the throat that says 'I'm old' or 'I'm young,' " for $3.00 and $5.00. These were prices for amounts of less than two ounces. The products were advertised modestly and in a rather undistinguished manner in narrow vertical columns in the back of some of the prestigious beauty magazines like *Vogue* and *Harper's Bazaar*.

Re-Nutriv, on the other hand, was very expensive, and that was precisely the point. Modeled after the very successful Orlane B-21, which sold for $75 for 2.5 ounces in Paris, Re-Nutriv went for $115 a pound.

Estée also manufactured, in limited editions, larger jars at hundreds of dollars and presented them like Fabergé Easter eggs. These larger jars were also given as bonuses to the saleswomen who had moved the most Re-Nutriv.

She went out and sold it herself at the more important department stores, grabbing her customer by the hand to implore, "You *have* to have this."

Re-Nutriv seems to have been the celebration of the million-dollar mark that the company hit in 1960. Estée took her first full-page advertisement in *Harper's Bazaar*—*Vogue* in those years seemed to have taken fashion to mean threads—and the first ad was a beauty. It featured what was to become the Lauder look. The model was elegant, with high cheekbones, and the glacial purity of a Hitchcock heroine.

The copy headline, of course:

WHAT MAKES A CREAM WORTH $115.00?
Re-Nutriv by Estée Lauder: Rare ingredients. Rare Formula. But above all the rare perception of a woman like Estée Lauder who knows almost better than anyone how to keep you looking younger, fresher, lovelier than you ever dreamed possible. She has created what she likes to think of as "a goldmine of beauty"—her Crème of Creams Re-Nutriv.

The ad went on to list *some* of these "costliest" ingredients: turtle oil, royal jelly, silicone, and leicol. Then there were the 20 *additional ingredients never before blended into one jar of cream.* Together these "youth-giving agents help rebuild and firm the skin, reflecting the freshness and radiance of a years-younger complexion.

Wisely, she remained within the fire-free zone: no specific attribution of any ingredient to any miracle, no claim medical enough to inculpate. Tony Liebler, who was in charge of getting Re-Nutriv into the stores and of watching over the merchandising of it once it got there, was impressed with the Lauders' attention to quality. "When they launch something," he says, "everything is done right." He calls Estée "ahead of her time for what was then the vagueness of her claims."

Was it worth the price?

"It was a good cream," Liebler waffles, "in terms of what is called its ability to penetrate. Not greasy. It left a nice feeling on the skin."

Re-Nutriv was a star product. The price made a point, it drew some attention and a little of what they call "free ink" in the trade; having first compelled attention, other less expensive products spun off it, lines within the line; more affordable lipsticks, makeup, everything but wire hangers.

There was even some indication that she was maybe beginning to be noticed by the royalty of the business.

Madame Helena Rubinstein put out something called Ultra Feminine Face Cream. She advertised it in *The New York Times* of January 3, 1960, standing hand-on-hip, eyeball-to-eyeball with a statue of the Venus de Milo, underneath which a caption asserted: "The same female hormones found in Ultra Feminine Face Cream gave Venus her form." (No mention made of who did her nails.) When Madame was asked why some of her latest creams were not doing as well as she had hoped (the product was selling regularly for $5.50, presumably for an ounce), she replied, "Not expensive enough."

The twenty secret ingredients to which the Re-Nutriv copy referred were, in fact, secret ingredients, even within the Lauder company. The basic cream was made in the Lauder lab in Nassau County under the supervision of a tall, baldish chemist named Vincent Basmajian. An unprepossessing man who read his yearly company-picnic speech haltingly from index cards, even *he*, they said, who'd been with the company forever, had no knowledge of the secret twenty.

He made the cream *around* the secret ingredients, then Joseph Lauder added the "never before blended into one jar of cream" agents. The formula itself was locked up in a vault, to which only he and Estée and Leonard had access. Tony Liebler was told it was the original family formula, handed down from the Viennese uncle.

In those days, Estée Lauder, Inc. had its headquarters at 666 Fifth Avenue, on the second floor. Estée was afraid of heights. She wouldn't take elevators, and she avoided airplanes. And at this time, she was beginning to become more and more fashion-conscious, beginning to think seriously and studiously about couture. Taste in clothes was not instinctive to her, and she had a hard, busty body to dress. Her very good friend, designer Jo Copeland, who once snapped at her, "Don't they have *mirrors* where you bought that dress?" gave her some advice. Estée began to sail to Paris several times a year to see the collections. Her small but burgeoning staff saw her off at each embarkment.

Many of the people taken on by Lauder at about this time would remain with the company for decades: Ida Steward, a tall, attractive southerner from Bristol-Myers, was called many things, but she was basically Estée's good right arm; June Leaman, from Bergdorf Goodman, would write and oversee all of the Estée Lauder advertising copy, even when the company affiliated itself with an advertising agency; Ira Levy, a fine-arts student at the University of California at Los Angeles by way of Helen van Slyke, was a young aesthetic genius whisked away by Estée. He would change her packaging from brown paper to tortoise shell. He would eventually travel the world in search of inspiration. His judgment would be *crucial* to Estée, and even extended to her clothes and the decoration of her houses. It wasn't until Ira came along that she began to trust someone *outside* the family. She wanted all kinds of advice in matters of taste, and Ira contributed brilliantly, unstintingly.

Before Ira, there had been a young man named Richard Chippler. Many people credit him with the early Lauder look; Bob Barnes came in as regional sales manager and would soon, along with Leonard, become responsible for the day-to-day running of Estée Lauder, Inc; George Friedman would come in to run the men's division and would leave because the family nature of the business limited his possibilities.

Those who stayed for the long haul would develop little fiefdoms. They had in common enormous talent, a personal dedication to the company, and a willingness to maintain a personal and professional reserve, an acknowledgment that there was *one* star and only one star in the company.

When the company was still at 666 Fifth Avenue, the staff participated in many aspects of Estée Lauder's life, there being little distinction drawn between bottom-line growth and the social elevation of the boss. So it was that the art department, every year, created a Christmas card for her that was supposed to look as if it had been done by Tiffany, only better. Andy Lucarelli, who was overseeing the preparation of the card one year, was called, on a Saturday morning, to Mrs. Lauder's home by Ida Steward. Mrs. Steward opened the door to Lucarelli, who was waiting for his employer to appear. She descended the steps of the town house, Christmas card held aloft.

"Look at this," she ordered Lucarelli.

"I'm looking," he responded.

"I wouldn't send this card to my maid," Estée shouted.

She pointed out to him that he had neglected to replicate the Tiffany embossment.

"This card is better and finer than anything we've ever done," Lucarelli insisted. "But I wouldn't do that for you; it's not right."

Lucarelli left the house and failed to report to work the next morning. Leonard went to his house to apologize for the incident. But things between him and Mrs. Lauder were never the same again, Lucarelli maintains. And he finally left Lauder with several other employees to form a cosmetic company with Zsa Zsa Gabor.

Industry giant Charles Revson, who was not afraid of the elevators but complained constantly of their slowness, inhabited the top floors at 666 Fifth Avenue. His staff had taken to calling the building sick-sick-sick. Revson hated the structure altogether, complaining that it had "metal bumps up and down the side, like pimples."

Helena Rubinstein maintained offices right across the street. She was terrified of Revson and of the enormous growth his company had undergone when he sponsored television's "The $64,000 Question." (Revlon had gone public in 1955 at $12 a share. Six months later, only weeks after the hit television quiz show debuted, the stock hit $30. And by mid-1956, it split.) Madame Rubinstein had been offered the show first and had refused it. "Only poor people watch those awful machines," she said. Although Estée's Re-Nutriv may have been worth a passing, imperious glance, the chief object of Madame's scorn was Revson. She could see the Revson offices from her own domain. And she would stare furiously at the building, muttering, "The Nail Man's busy in there, copying us. . . . I swear!"

Estée had no desire to take on the Nail Man, her co-tenant. Once during the early stages of his career, Leonard had the idea that Lauder should begin to produce nail lacquer. There had been

Eczema Ointment of John Schotz. (*Photo courtesy of the private collection of Lucille Carlan Rottkov*)

Estée's childhood home in Corona, Queens.

Public School 14, which Estée attended.

The Gottlieb Cottage, Delafield, Wisconsin. *(Courtesy of Jane Abbott; photo by Ed Beyler)*

From left to right: John Schotz, Ole Olsen (of Olsen and Johnson comedy fame), Dorraine Dupont, and two unidentified friends.

Elizabeth Arden in 1922. Arden was one of Estée's chief rivals.
(*UPI/Bettmann Newsphotos*)

Opposite: Estée Lauder, circa 1962. (*UPI/Bettmann Newsph*

A. L. van Ameringen, former head of
International Flavors and Fragrances.
(The New York Times)

Charles Revson, archrival of Estée's, with Charlotte Ford.
(*UPI/Bettmann Newsphotos*)

Lauder family members: from left to right, Joe, Estée, Ronald, and Ronald's wife, Jo Carole.

Leonard A. Lauder
(*AP/Wide World Photos*)

Karen Graham, model for Estée Lauder. (*AP/Wide World Photos*)

many requests for it. So he put a plan together and took it into Estée.

"I don't want to get started with him," she bristled. "No, I don't want to get started with him."

Him was, of course, Charles Revson, who had begun his multi-million-dollar empire with polish. "Right now Charles Revson is my friend," she explained to Leonard. "He doesn't take me seriously. . . . He thinks I'm a cute blond lady. . . . The moment I put something on the market that competes with him, he's going to get *upset*. He's going to get difficult. And we're not big enough to fight him."

She would deal instead with Palm Beach, a Florida resort community fourteen miles long and two miles wide. As she and Leonard were building her business, Palm Beach was where Estée intended to make it happen for herself socially, and it was a good and a wise choice. Everybody who was anybody stayed in or passed through or guested in Palm Beach; though it was rigidly stratified, it was porous. Like the wings of a butterfly.

Recently, a press agent explained the community in the restaurant of the Colony Hotel. "You see, the whole world comes to Palm Beach. And you have them right here in a nutshell all at once in a season. And when you entertain those people here, they're going to reciprocate when they're back where they came from: Europe, the south of France. And press? You do things here and it goes *right* up to Suzy. There are good names, good people, good reasons for parties. And you can meet people here as you can never meet them in their own bailiwick. It's all in one wonderful round big ball. And it's all so relaxed."

Estée bought her first house in Palm Beach in the late fifties. It was a small Spanish house on Route Trail, described by a local savant as "the least desirable neighborhood—the ghetto." By 1964 she had a better place—a showcase even by Palm Beach standards, a creamy villa. It was described by a public relations person: "Georgian. You go down to the ocean and you have to make a left. I was in that house when it was owned by Mrs. Swenson. Ed Swenson's mother, of the First National Bank of Miami. Mrs. Swenson was in a wheelchair. She died, and Estée bought the house—full of eighteenth-century English furniture. Swimming pool right on the ocean."

When Estée was beginning her climb there, Marjorie Merri-weather Post, mistress of the fabulous Mar-A-Lago, was ending her long reign as social queen bee, and Mary Sanford, mistress of the palatial Los Incas, was taking over. Mrs. Sanford was the plucky wife of Stephen (Laddie) Sanford, the whilom carpet magnate and horse breeder. Her big game was polo, and in the loggia of her house were mounted several hunting trophies, including a man-eating tiger that she shot herself. She carried a straw purse on which was written: "I thrive on Love, Leisure, and Luxury." Los Incas, by the sea, was so big that she allowed her eight Dobermans to romp, and boasted, "They never meet."

The leisure ladies of Palm Beach, many of them ex-show girls married to retired industrialists who in their time had invented some unassailably profitable industrial part, spent a good deal of their time and energy preparing galas, balls, fetes, and luncheons, the profits of which spilled over into their favorite charities. They ran the Annual Christmas Ball for the Animal Rescue League, the Polo Ball for the benefit of the Yale University polo team; the Society of St. Mary's Annual Luncheon; the Salvation Army Association's International Philanthropic Awards Dinner; the gala for Friends of the Bascom Palmer Eye Institute; and assorted fetes for diabetes, cancer, the DAR, the Red Cross, and Hope and Heart.

The way to bust these balls—Estée's way—was to contribute wonderful little baskets of Lauder products as party favors. One of Estée's first mentions in the *Palm Beach Daily News*, the so-called Shiny Sheet that watches the so-called Cottage Community the way Boswell watched Jonson, refers to the gala for the Palm Beach American Red Cross Ball of February 17, 1963. The

Shiny Sheet item read: "Favors donated by Mrs. Estée Lauder. Mrs. Estée Lauder is president of the cosmetic company that bears her name." Estée began contributing regularly to the party scene. She was a generous and canny giver. And even when Estée was not herself at the ball, her presents were felt.

Which did not mean that she was invited to dinner parties. Or that she became overnight in any way acceptable within the Cottage Community. Or that her bounteous gift-giving was always effective. Mary Sanford recalls that she was once persuaded by Estée to take her to dinner at the home of Dorothy Munn. Dorothy Munn was the wife of financier Charles Munn, whom *Newsweek* had designated as "Old Guard" in a taxonomic breakdown of Palm Beach society in 1966. Old Guard led their list vis-à-vis invincibility. Other categories were "corporate," "philanthropic," "young and jetty," "very social," and, finally, "theatrical" ("drop-ins like Joan Crawford"). Estée showed up at Mrs. Munn's bearing gifts. Mary Sanford remembers the occasion with a kind of incredulity: "She gave Dorothy Munn, who is a great heiress, a great big box full of *cosmetics*! And Mrs. Munn said, 'She must be crazy!' Mrs. Munn had her cosmetics made privately. What did she do? Well, she *almost* gave them back."

Another possible way to pierce or try to pierce Palm Beach was through the local art galleries, which were social hubs of the community. Estée began buying paintings from George Vigoreux. Vigoreux was the uncle of playwright Edward Albee, and he ran a gallery that was backed by Joan Whitney Payson and Mary Sanford. He used to throw lavish mainstream parties, many of which were attended by C. Z. Guest, the extremely social wife of Winston Guest, heir to the Phipps fortune and cousin to Winston Churchill. Estée knew about the parties, understood that they were attended by C. Z. Guest, and, one day, simply asked Vigoreux if she could come, reminding him that she had dropped a lot of bucks on his Dufys. Mrs. Guest, who had been in show business as a Vanities girl, did not then have too many

Jewish friends and she resisted the idea of attending a party with Estée Lauder.

"Estée had always wanted to meet C. Z. Guest," observed a prominent public-relations person who knows the Palm Beach beat. "She used to stop at C. Z.'s table at La Grenouille in New York to tell her that she was the most beautiful woman in the room. To Estée, C. Z. was social, inaccessible, and elegant. She wanted desperately to know her and she did *finally* sort of beguile her."

Estée, a combination vortical force, jack-in-the-box, hard-scrabble seller, went out of her way to court several securely entrenched, awfully Christian Palm Beach personae. Jean Tailer was another. At the Poinciana Club, in 1985, a local impresario explains Jean Tailer, et al.: "She's Tommy's wife, T. Suffern Tailer. Handsome guy, beautiful personality. He was a bulwark here socially. He was Newport, Tuxedo Park—in other words, the top of the line. Jean was his wife. Tommy ended up with not too much money, having lived beautifully, *as a gentleman*. And Estée hired Jean Tailer. Maybe a softer word than hired; to do a lot of work to *promote* and so forth. Top girls, Jean and C. Z. I think they did her a lot of good."

A lot of them were beguiled by Estée's intrepidity. Mary Sanford examined her own feelings about Estée: "She courted me and I was flattered. At charity benefits, she gave me presents. . . . She is *very* aggressive. Still is. So socially aggressive. You just wonder."

Lois Hagen of *The Milwaukee Journal* visited Estée's house on North Ocean Boulevard when Hagen was doing a series about "former Wisconsin residents" who had resort homes in Florida. Estée gave her the I-grew-up-in-Delafield-my-mother-was-so-beautiful-a-woman-came-in-every-day-just-to-brush-her-hair speech, showed her the Meissen urns, the Chippendale furniture, the sconces, and the silver plates. And Joe Lauder, whom Hagen called "a hospitable man with a quiet, easygoing manner," kept her and her photographer company while his wife changed.

Hagen remembers that Estée spent a lot of time changing clothes. Other people she had interviewed for the series dolled themselves up in one outfit and posed in different rooms. But Estée donned a breakfast ensemble for the breakfast room, a luncheon outfit for the luncheon room, and a long gown for her dinner pose.

At the end of the long and very exhausting session, Hagen and her photographer were ready to leave and return to their hotel. Estée asked the reporter, "Couldn't you stay awhile? We'll have someone drive your photographer back."

Alone now with Lois Hagen, Estée began a complete makeover on the reporter. "You know, I started out as a beautician and demonstrator," she assured her, "so I know what I'm doing." She creamed off the little bit of makeup that remained on Hagen after the long workday and deftly did her eyes, lips, cheeks. She then presented her with an "enormous kit" of Lauder products, and said her goodbyes. Hagen was thrilled. "I didn't look like myself when she finished, but I looked real good. I went to meet the photographer for dinner and he didn't recognize me. And I was hooked on the products. I wore only Lauder cosmetics for years."

6

REVSON'S FOLLY

The competition was dying. First, on April Fool's Day, in 1965, Helena Rubinstein, or Princess Gourielli (she had actually been married to a Georgian prince), succumbed. After suffering several strokes she drifted off into what her loving biographer, Patrick O'Higgins, hoped was a "swift reincarnation." Just the year before she had been robbed in her Manhattan triplex by three men in the early morning. They had followed her butler, Albert, into her bedroom. She was abed, expecting breakfast, and nonplussed by their entrance: she thought they were lawyers. One of the thieves demanded the keys to her safe. "I'm an old woman," she replied. "You can kill me. But I'm not going to let you rob me. Now get out!"

They upended her purse and fled with one hundred dollars in cash. Overlooked were the forty-thousand-dollar earrings that had tumbled out of the purse, the Picassos and Braques on the walls, and gems lying about haphazardly.

She was ninety-three or older when she died. The company, already public in part, was sold to Colgate, which marketed her products like soap.

A year later, at eighty-one or eighty-four, Elizabeth Arden was dead. Tiny, just like Madame Rubinstein, she wore little flowered hats and carried an alligator handbag even in her own living room. She was an imperious, volatile, neurotic woman. Once she fired a line girl for sneezing. Mostly, she cared about the thoroughbred horses she maintained at her Main Chance Farm in Lexington, Kentucky. She had a Derby winner, Jet Pilot, in 1947. Her real name was Florence Nightingale Graham; she used the name Mrs. Elizabeth N. Graham in the racing world. She talked baby talk to her horses, piped music into their stalls, and had them massaged with Elizabeth Arden Eight Hour Cream and Ardena Skin Lotion. She left her multimillion-dollar empire in disarray. It, too, went to the highest bidder.

There had been a bitter rivalry between Arden and Rubinstein. According to Margaret Allen, in *Selling Dreams*, the rivalry obtained not in the "copying of each other's products—both ranges of cosmetics sold well and made a profit—but in the behavior of the two women. They never referred to each other by name; it was always 'that woman' or 'the other one.' " They pirated each others' people. Once Arden almost cleaned house at Rubinstein. "Rubinstein retaliated by taking on Arden's ex-husband, Thomas Lewis." They were never invited to the same party, and each maintained she had never met the other one. Each claimed to be the world's leading beauty expert and there was something to be said for both claims. Between 1915 and 1920, Arden was the biggest cosmetics manufacturer extant. Rubinstein is credited with having been the first to temper her creams to the variety of complexion needs: oily, dry, and something in-between.

Socially, they had entirely different areas of dominance. Madame Rubinstein, the Jewish princess, for all her crude behavior—she blew her nose in her silk bedsheets, she gobbled Polish sausage, she called her competitors' products "drek"—was accepted everywhere. Her clothes were garish and completely sui generis. *"Qui est la tireuse de cartes?* ("Who's the fortune-teller?") a taxi driver once asked Patrick O'Higgins when he and Madame were driving through the hills above Cannes. The community they were passing over, La Californie, was Estée's first neighborhood in the south of France. "Very Jewish," Madame Rubinstein traduced. Withal, she was a true internationalist, at home with Coco Chanel, Golda Meir, the Duke and Duchess of Windsor, and Jean Cocteau. Her art collection and her jewels were an unselfconscious testament to the prodigal eclecticism, a love of all things ebulliently visual.

Though Arden was born in Canada, the daughter of a truck driver, she was more at home in the United States. Her love of horses, her hats, her tea parties, and her vocal anti-Semitism gave her a social acceptance in those citadels and sanctuaries of WASP America for which Estée hungered. A woman who worked for Miss Arden for decades and was pampered by her like a thoroughbred remembers, "I wanted to get married years ago and Elizabeth Arden said, 'Don't get married! I don't want you to get married! I'll send you to Europe to live!' Well, I was on my *honeymoon* and she telephoned me and I had to leave for Main Chance the second day of my honeymoon. . . . She used to *ship* my car to Florida. Was afraid of my driving. Afraid something would happen to me . . . But class! We had tea in the afternoon with maid service for the buyers. Oh, what class! Estée could never be the *lady* that Miss Arden was."

The demise of her sister entrepreneurs gave Estée, among other things, a kind of iconographic edge. This was a time when fashion-merchant personalities were beginning to attract more and more press attention. *Women's Wear Daily* was just starting to report on the world of cosmetics on a weekly basis; Palm Beach stringers, and finally some of their own most vital writers, were covering the mix-and-match world of society cum merchants. Estée's Palm Beach plan paid dividends. Bob Wirtz, an executive who was with Lauder in the mid-sixties, observes, "There was *no way* when Estée started that she had the budget to compete with the Revlons of the world—or the Germaine Monteils, or the Frances Denneys, and a lot of them have gone by the wayside. But she kept going up and up. There was something about Estée that drew what we call free ink, publicity. She was always at the right place at the right time. And she had a flair for making people like her, whereas some of the other cosmetic giants had a flair for making people absolutely detest them."

Among the most detested was Charles Revson, under whose skin (which Helena Rubinstein had observed to be dry), Estée Lauder was beginning to get. And she nettled him long before she should have been considered as anything but a gadfly.

Emperor of Revlon, Charles Revson had been top of the line and top of the world for decades. The profit column of his business, as reported by his *Fire and Ice* biographer Andrew Tobias, was astounding. The business, which started as nail polish, had yielded him a salary of $16,500 in 1937, when Estée was peddling her uncle's cream. Revson added lipstick to his line in 1940; total sales shot up to $2.8 million. Those sales, according to Tobias, sextupled in the forties, septupled in the fifties, and nearly tripled in the sixties.

Although Estée's company was growing by leaps and bounds, she was still doing only an estimated $14 million in 1965. Revlon was head and shoulders above the Lauder organization as to bottom line, and even department stores and classy stores. *Women's Wear Daily* reported in 1969 that Revlon was in 15,000 stores versus Lauder's approximate 1,200.

Yes, there were inroads here, incursions there, and small triumphs in real estate, but what really got to Revson, it would appear, was Estée's social obsession. He thought he had her number, mainly because they had so much in common. Each was the child of Jewish immigrants; Revson's father was a Russian Jew who rolled cigars in Manchester, Massachusetts. Neither one had gone any further than high school. Each started a business with nothing but genius; both were singularly obsessed with business. And neither one of them ever recognized any other piggy's right to go to market.

"*Of course* the other guy has a right to make a living," Revson is quoted by Tobias to have conceded, "but let him make it in some other business."

Despite their notable salesmanship, neither one of them was anything *approaching* articulate. Both rambled. Revson's verbal logjams were well chronicled in Andrew Tobias's *Fire and Ice.* Estée's articulations defy recapitulation. She doesn't think like other people or talk like them either. She is memorable but not *memorizable.* People tend to remember her configurationally, never word for word. A Lauder executive recalls her conducting a business meeting: "Estée's genius? Five different products on the table and she would start talking, *almost rambling.* But in her dialogue there would be *absolute gems . . .* I would have a difficult time remembering why she wanted a box gold instead of blue, but the reason was really a brilliant reason that nobody else would have thought of."

Revson did several things about this woman, no longer just a cute blond lady. He railed. To Harry Doyle, his charming, affable employee, whom he would ask to head up the Princess Borghese line, Revson bristled: "Goddamn it, Harry, her name's not Estée. It's Esther. Esther-from-Brooklyn!"

And he began to copy her. Revson had never made a secret of his predeliction to copy; it was a technique of his. Mike Sager, who worked for a time as Revson's West Coast representative, is reported to have been told by his boss, "Copy everything and you can't go wrong." Tobias asserts that this was Revson's formula for four decades: "That way you let the competitors do the groundwork and make the mistakes. And when they hit with something good, you make it better, package it better, advertise it better, and bury them."

When Lauder brought out a line of twenty-one products for men in 1965 called Aramis, he brought out a line of products for men in 1966 called Braggi; when she began most effectively to use black-and-white print ads, primarily because she could not afford color, he followed suit. Harry Doyle recalls, "He tried to copy the Lauder advertising by doing gravure. Revson didn't like black-and-white, he liked color. But he saw the black-and-white and he asked, 'What can we do?' So we went to gravure. It's amazing, you take one step back and you're no longer the class act. Somebody else is the class act."

Estée was not amused. She told Marilyn Bender of *The New York Times*: "He even stole our tortoise paper from Aramis. Everybody copies somebody, but everybody can change it. Even if I copy, nobody knows I copy. There had been bath oils before I made my bath oil into a fragrance."

The popular slogan at the Lauder offices became "50 percent of Revlon's R&D is done here."

Revson had seemed, way back, much larger than he really was because he advertised so extensively. When his company was a couple of small rooms in 1935, he spent $335.56, the total annual advertising budget, on one cock-and-bull promotion in *The New Yorker* magazine. He borrowed to advertise; he plowed an unseemly percentage of his profits back into advertising.

His incredibly exciting campaigns for matching lipstick and nail polish—the so-called Fire and Ice promotions—began in the fall of 1952, and they were a sensation. Schoolgirls waited for his new fall colors—each of which would obsolesce its predecessor— the way their fathers waited for the new Buick. *Business Week* called his sultry advertising look "one of the most effective ads in cosmetics history." By 1975, he was spending an estimated $65 million annually. And advertising continued to be his strongest suit even when he was foolish enough, on occasion, to mess up his genius by emulating the muted Lauder look.

Estée's trick with mirrors continued to be social elevation. It was no less a basic drive because it served her so well professionally. She was insatiable; she could never get enough. She set her social sights higher and higher.

There was a time when, even in *this* regard, his heart never really in it, Charles Revson—ostensibly to beat Estée at her own game and thereby to beat the drum for his own imitative, prestige lines—tried to make the social scene. He had always rented or owned yachts and lived life lavishly, but he had never used his wealth to acquire either cachet or the kinds of people who could imbue him with it. He was not even inclined to surround himself with peers, opting for henchmen and beautiful women.

After he married young Lyn Fisher Sheresky in 1964—some say primarily on account of that marriage and not so much in response to Estée—foul-mouthed, irascible Revlon began to mobilize. He and Lyn, both in yachting white, posed for *Town & Country* magazine on his recently purchased *Ultima I*, the third largest private yacht in the world. He invited columnist Eugenia Sheppard and Mildred Custin of Bonwit's aboard. Lyn began appearing on Eleanor Lambert's best-dressed lists, though she denied, of course, being represented by Lambert.

He purchased the magnificent Park Avenue triplex in which Madame Rubinstein had resided at the time of her death and made one whole floor into a ballroom and threw lavish balls and dinner parties. However, he had little talent or toleration for the game. He would tell his former wife, Ancky Johnson, with whom he remained on good terms ("Divorcing Charles Revson was the greatest mistake in my life," Ancky says) that he was *on* to the kind of people who came to his parties and ate his food and drank his booze and hated his guts.

He lacked the grace and the hypocrisy to play the subsidiary game, although he wanted the lion's share of the class market on which Estée was focusing. He wanted it so much that, according to a Revlon executive quoted in *Fire and Ice*, "his priorities came all out of whack. The whole corporation was working on one percent of its business ninety percent of the time to satisfy this ego of his."

Ironically, that ego of his was precisely what militated against his playing endurably or well the escalation game at which Estée excelled.

There was no couple more ne plus ultra in the sixties than the Duke and Duchess of Windsor. Palm Beach was so crazy about them (they had begun sojourning there when he was serving as the governor and commander-in-chief of the Bahamas) the social set even named a season after them. "The little season" was the time in April when people extended their normal stay so that they might possibly be in the company of the ex-King and his fashionable wife; for this was the time that they came to hully gully. "Wherever the Duke and Duchess go, the world goes," Elsa Maxwell had written shortly before her death.

For a time, during their annual visits, they had stayed at the swank Colony Hotel. Then they were lured away by various ardent hosts. Mrs. Robert R. Young had them for a time. She was the widow of a railroad tycoon who had committed suicide because he had reckoned himself broke. He had, in fact, miscalculated. With part of the six million dollars that had been somehow overlooked, Anita Young built a big house with a heated swimming pool and retractable chandeliers, primarily to entertain the royal duo. In 1966 they were staying with Arthur and Susie Gardner—he had been the United States Ambassador to Cuba.

Estée was absolutely smitten by the fashion-plate Duchess, despite the fact that the Duchess, wrinkle-free in her mid-seventies, frequently credited Erno Laszlo as the "guardian of my skin." Estée had blitzed the Duchess with Lauder lipstick. Once the Duchess wrote her a gracious little note in which she indicated that her supply had reached the point of glut and that perhaps Estée should, for the nonce, forbear. Estée had called her, in print, "the most attractive woman in the world." But lipsticks and accolades were not enough to woo the Duchess.

Stories abound explaining how it was that Estée Lauder finally

acquired the couple. Common gossip in Palm Beach had Estée
making an outright payment to them of $25,000. That is un-
likely. Even their most critical biographer, Charles Murphy, re-
futes the idea that they were, at any time, outright bribable. The
Duke was not a poor man and he was, furthermore, a proud one.
They were not, however, averse to perks. In return for his presence in a game of golf, he would accept a wise investment tip. For
mentioning a ship, a hotel, a Dior, a Balmain—or even the
guardian of her skin—there were hefty discounts given. And
there would come a time when Estée Lauder would have the
privilege of giving the Windsors' annual anniversary dinner.

Estée told Marilyn Bender that she and the Windsors actually
met at sea aboard the S.S. *United States*, that the Duchess asked to
meet her because she had been using the Lauder line for years and
that Youth-Dew was the *only* fragrance the Duke liked: "They
had cocktails together and the friendship ripened in Palm Beach,
Paris, and other points distant from West End Avenue."

Now they could, in fact, have drunk together on the high seas,
but, according to another source, their first real meeting was on
the flat tracks, and it was instigated, orchestrated, and carefully
set up by Estée as the end of the 1966 little season was drawing to
a close.

Estée knew that, like herself, the Duchess was afraid to fly and
that she customarily returned to New York by train. Using a
bevy of carefully cultivated connections, including an employee
at the tiny West Palm railroad station, Estée ascertained the date
and time of the Windsors' impending departure and the precise
location of the private railroad car that the couple had booked a
week in advance.

Accordingly, she booked passage for Joe and herself aboard the
Florida Special bound for New York Friday night, April 15.

The fretful Windsors, both nervous travelers, pulled into the
quiet West Palm station with their pet pug, Ambassador, and
Mrs. Gardner, and a man called "Doc" Holden; a station wagon

followed, which held their thirty-odd pieces of luggage and the special food the Ambassador's chef had prepared for the royal couple. The Duchess wore a smart suit, an orchid, white gloves, and a chiffon scarf around her head. The Duke was impeccably tailored, with a sporty silk-lined fedora.

In seconds, the Lauders' car pulled in. The Duke and Duchess sat fitfully in their air-conditioned limo, the door ajar. Estée, in a light suit, somewhat rumpled in the seat, pocketbook suspended from her arm, approached the Windsors' car.

"Oh, are you taking the train, also?" she asked.

A photographer, who had been tipped off by the station employee, was on hand to record the event. There was a shot of Estée and the Duchess, Estée's gloved hand on the Duchess's somewhat stiff elbow.

The picture of the cosmetics queen and the exilic Duchess appeared on the front page of the Shiny Sheet, and it went out on the wire. Estée saw to that.

They had almost two days alone together aboard the northbound *Florida Special* to get acquainted. Thus was begun the landmark relationship that established Estée Lauder as a redoubtable force on the social scene.

7

CLINIQUE

The idea of the Lauder woman, of using the same model over a period of time to symbolize Estée's fantasy of the gracious, good life, to personify the company, to tell the customer what the Lauder product might do for her, had originated back in 1962 when there were no more than a dozen people on staff.

A young photographer from Chicago, Victor Skrebneski, had taken a picture of chinchilla-clad Phyllis Connor, a housewife/model also from Chicago. The photo was black and white. As a child Skrebneski had gone almost daily to the movies and he would watch repeatedly the black-and-white films from France that featured Michele Morgan, Jean Marais, and Simone Simon. He wrote in a collection of portraits that would be published in 1978: "All the films were in black and white. Black blacks, blinding whites, and soft grays. Later, I was excited but disappointed to see my first color film . . . I had accepted film stars as real—color made them unreal."

This picture of Phyllis Connor—which had been shown to the Lauder staff when Richard Chippler was the art director—was influenced by the French import *Last Year at Marienbad*, a visually stunning movie in which Delphine Seyrig, smoothly coifed, stared at a great deal of dazzling topiary.

Leonard saw the Skrebneski picture and said, Eureka, that's the look we want. And we want it in black and white because we can't afford color. Estée thought the pictures were not as good as

68

they could be. She was right: The first Skrebneskis were not as good as they would finally become.

The early advertisements were created without the help of an outside advertising agency. Skrebneski worked with June Leaman. Shoots were done in Skrebneski's coach house in an urban renewal area of Chicago's North Side—using his own travertine floors and Lalique ashtrays, and eighteenth-century Chinese scroll-back chairs. It was not until the mid-sixties that the Lauders began to use an agency called AC&R, the infant fledgling of Ted Bates. Lauder was their first client. The chief people there were Alvin Chereskin, a Brooklyn boy who had started on the marketing side of Revlon and Rubinstein, and Lou Miano, who came over from feature writing at *Show* and *Look* magazines.

When Estée's higher-priced fragrances were introduced, Skrebneski pulled back his camera, widening the shot to show not only the woman but the way she lived, among Ming vases, chinoiseries, pre-Columbian art, oriental rugs, or Picasso ceramics.

June Leaman, who wrote the words to Skrebneski's music, described the one and only image; the image of Estée Lauder products: "She has the confident look of a woman with the world in the palm of her hand. Seeing her in the Estée Lauder world, you somehow know that her closets are impeccable, her children well-behaved, her husband devoted, and her guests pampered."

That was Estée's fantasy, felicitously introjected. Indeed, the look became so integral a part of the company that later there would be people who thought that Karen Graham, the most successful of the Lauder women, was in fact Estée Lauder herself. Karen Graham reigned elegantly for fifteen years as Lauder's only model, in print advertisements and on television.

With all the pride and the passion that Estée had invested in her name and that image, she had the good sense and the acumen to go with the flow of the late sixties, and, in the process, to open a floodgate or two of her own. The claim again was in the name:

Clinique. It connoted a world and a sensibility entirely different from the privileged, languorous image of the Lauder woman and the world she inhabited. Clinique was a line of products created for a younger generation of women to whom beauty was less embellishment than fitness, health, and good caretaking.

The new line comprised therapeutic skin care, marketed and advertised with absolutely no reference to Estée. That it was her company remained a trade secret, known to the several thousand people in the business, in the same way that the IFF connection was known only to insiders.

Leonard Lauder has only recently admitted, in a speech before an organization of women executives, that the idea was his and that it came out of a self-induced challenge: "The most formidable competition that you can conjure up is yourselves and something you dream up yourself. . . . The reason we launched Clinique is that I felt that if I were going to go into business against Estée Lauder this is exactly how I would do it."

The Lauder press spiel attributes the beginnings of Clinique to a piece that ran in the August 15, 1967, *Vogue*. The cover line for the putative inspiration was: "GREAT SKIN—A Dermatologist Tells When It Can Be Created." The dermatologist, though not named then, was Dr. Norman Orentreich, a famous New York skin specialist. The format of the piece was question and answer. The questioner, also unnamed, was Carol Phillips, a *Vogue* staffer for twenty-six years at the time.

Phillips described the doctor as an "active research and clinical dermatologist . . . his office lively with the curiosity of a group of cosmetically minded physicians whose chief beat is skin." His clients, she explained, were "twenty-six-year-old models," who popped in for "skin refreshment," and "older people," learning that their "faces can deny their decade of birth, that time can be turned back, facially, gracefully."

The piece was well done; Phillips' questions covered all the bases and were spoken like a true veteran of *Vogue* who began there as a copywriter after graduating from the University of North Carolina. Orentreich's responses were pungent, responsible, and pregnant with futurity. He reeled off a rap of hopefulness that would lay the groundwork for the next twenty years of skin-care claims: The upper layer of older skin thins. Moisturizers and emollients help this layer hold water. "The film of cream on the skin helps prevent moisture loss . . . Eventually the under layer which is the supportive layer of the skin retains less water, too. If it can be induced to keep its moisture, it provides better support and plumps up wrinkled skin." Creams might "rejuvenate briefly . . . and enough brieflys add up to lengthilys."

For certain conditions there was nothing but surgery or derm-abrasion, but Orentreich was saying clearly that dermatologists were working on a broad spectrum of possibilities to turn back the clock by using topically applied, over-the-counter preparations.

Then he revealed the regimen he recommended to the young women who want to responsibly "caretaker" their skin. (There were no considerations yet that young men might be similarly inclined.) He told them to use soap and water; he believed in soap and water. But soap and water couldn't do it all. This should be followed by an astringent for "exfoliation"; certain astringents, he claimed, were better than others. Finally, he advocated a moisturizing lotion for lubrication.

He had, to all intents and purposes, laid out the Clinique blueprint of three products:

Clinique's dermatologists worked it out this way: 3 products, 3 steps, 3 minutes each morning and night. Clean with Clinique's great soap. Clear away with a clarifier for your skin type. Replenish with moisturizer. That's it. That's all.

These words would be written by Carol Phillips, who was apparently ready for a change anyway when Estée came courting. She had spent twelve years as managing editor of *Vogue* and had

71

presumably been passed over for the top spot as editor-in-chief after Diana Vreeland left. She was in her late forties, the mother of two grown children, divorced, a very private person whose home phone number was known to few people in her work environment. There were other offers besides Estée's; she claimed four the very week she made up her mind to go with Lauder. Revlon's brilliant copywriter, Kay Daly, was taking her to lunch and offering her more money than Estée. But Estée, again, would not take no for an answer. And there was more than one lunch.

"So you're coming to work with us," Estée said.

And Carol Phillips would answer, "No, I haven't told you that."

She did finally go with Lauder, so compelling was Estée's salesmanship and so intriguing the challenge of *developing* and overseeing a brand-new line of products, modestly priced, for the no-nonsense youth market. She joined Estée Lauder, Inc. in December 1967, continuing to work closely with Dr. Orentreich, who formulated the line. She was called *directrice*.

The line was touted as "allergy-tested, fragrance-free." The term "hypo-allergenic" would yo-yo in and out of the Clinique presentation over the years. The FDA clearly did not like the term; it was too medical-sounding for a cosmetic claim. The agency asked for certain quantitative standards. A consortium of companies, including Almay and Lauder, fought for the right to maintain the word and won. Nonetheless, Clinique stayed more or less with "allergy-tested"; it was problem-free and, besides, it scanned better.

The idea of ferreting out allergens from cosmetics products was not a new one. In the early thirties, Marcelle Cosmetics had been permitted to advertise in the *Journal of the American Medical Association* because they had screened out many of the potentially irritating substances in their products. Almay and Ar-Ex offered to disclose the contents of any of their products upon request, before such disclosure was mandated by a law that Lauder and all the major producers fought.

The fragrance-free idea was not a new one either. The essential oils of many fragrances are among the most irritating of cosmetic substances; so the idea went hand-in-glove with the screening process. The lack of odor was achieved, ironically, by adding a chemical masking agent to neutralize the noisomeness of the other chemicals. But it did not make the Clinique products purer. It was simply another clinical affectation—Clinique's very odorlessness is itself a kind of odor, like the ozone layer in a rain forest.

The early producers of hypo-allergenic fragrance-free products were offering simple products for simple needs at modest prices. Clinique was, however, to be more than a regimen of unembellished products. It was to be total environment: a tintinnabulation of product, marketing, advertising, push, patience, and theater. Lauder/Clinique would ring them bells.

Most of it happened at the counter. The FDA was, to some extent, able to prevent Clinique from making medical-*sounding* claims. But there was no law on earth that prevented them from *looking* as medical as they bloody well pleased. The salespeople (all women in the beginning) are referred to as "consultants." They are done up in white lab coats. And the space in which they work—at a far remove from the Estée Lauder area—is suffused with fluorescent lighting. The products are packaged entirely in a faint green, more antiseptic than minty. And customers are directed to a color-coded Clinique computer—called a Ouija board by competitors—into which they feed answers to questions about the oiliness or dryness of their skin; the computer spits back recommendations about which Clinique products to use.

The first consultants who sold the Clinique line were rigorously trained and overseen by twenty staff supervisors who traveled around the country, often appearing on radio and television. Some of them went on to executive positions within the company.

The headquarters from which Carol Phillips ran Clinique, after the entire organization moved to the General Motors building in 1968, was predictably antiseptic: white tiles, white walls—none of the frou-frou Louis's of the Lauder layout.

Clinique spends very little on advertising. The push is at the counter. What they choose to do, however, is first rate. The Lauder/Clinique people seldom win awards; the company is too politically unpopular. But Clinique advertising is acknowledged among people in the field as nonpareil, a classic in the field of print advertising. The original photographer was Irving Penn; the very same advertisement that ran in *The New York Times Magazine* in 1974 still runs, unchanged, in 1985.

The advertisement shows a toothbrush leaning in a glass and the words, "twice a day"—the obvious inference being that the Clinique regimen is as simple and as quotidian as the toothbrush habit. Another of Penn's classics, when Clinique later expanded to include products for men, is a medicine cabinet full of the greatly elaborated crop of Clinique, again indicating the necessity of the line.

The consummate touch was the Penn photography. Using primitive equipment and printing on paper hand-coated with platinum instead of silver—he professed a preference for shooting things rather than people—Penn's photos have a range of tones, a humor, and an immanence quite unlike that of any other artist in the field. John Szarkowski, director of the department of photography at the Museum of Modern Art in Manhattan, has referred to Penn's ability to render the "idiosyncratic humors of light," of his awareness that "the apparently inconsequential can be redeemed by artistic seriousness; that a plain vocabulary is the most demanding; that high craft is the just dessert not only of museums and ceremonial vessels, but of the ordinary baggage of our lives."

Leonard Lauder is said not to have liked the toothbrush ad in the beginning. Estée might have had nothing at all to do with it. It was perhaps Carol Phillips's notion to run with Penn. He had come to them with more than adequate credentials, having been art director at Saks. He had also worked for *Vogue*; he photographed their first black-and-white cover.

No matter who had had the first or the final say about Penn's unique and rather daring photography, it was the genius of the Lauder organization to use the work in the first place and to resist changing it for ten years. Good taste, good luck, or superstitiousness (Mrs. Lauder knocks on wood a lot, and an advertising man named Marvin Davis, who worked with the company briefly in the 1970s, compared the Lauders to a baseball team on a winning streak afraid to change their uniforms), the Irving Penn art is a sterling example of both the flexibility and the prudency of a company of Luddites, aesthetes, and brilliant merchandisers.

Clinique lost $3 million before it hit really big in 1975. *Forbes* magazine claimed in 1981, by which time the company was called the "walkaway leader" in its field, that "the people who bought Clinique like the scientific therapeutic attitude behind it. That was costly, but the Lauders spent the money, took the losses for a while and nourished the business."

There were other major competitive launches, including Revlon's unsuccessful copy of Clinique, Etherea. Andrew Tobias details the Etherea fiasco in *Fire and Ice*, reporting that Revson had returned home from a summer cruise and that he had "a fit" when he learned Estée's hypo-allergenic line was out; he claimed to have been thinking about bringing out such a group of products for three years. He then geared up his company to produce a complete line in seven months—names, packaging, products, the works. He promised Mildred Custin of Bonwit Teller delivery on April 28. There followed a series of panics, fiascoes, embarrassments, with the company flying by the seat of its pants, working seven days a week, with executives delivering the products personally in station wagons, making skid marks through department store aisles. Revson lost this one for his slipshodness and because department stores were beginning to grant Lauder the edge on account of its exclusivity: Revlon's products could be purchased all over. The buyer at a midwestern department store explained to *Forbes*: "Some stores aren't interested in building Revlon skin-care sales because the customer doesn't have to come back to us to buy the product again. She can go to a discounter and get the same stuff for less."

Conversely, Clinique remained exceedingly patient, provident, and exclusive. As late as 1983, Clinique products were sold in only 287 stores in the United States, totaling 1,700 doors. Phillips never sacrificed quality and service. She told *Women's Wear Daily*, "We have a report on every single person who sells Clinique in any store in this country. If we see someone is selling $140 worth of products every time she makes a sale, then something is wrong. She's loading—putting too much pressure on the customers."

Only a private company could have tolerated such prudent adventurism. And Lauder remained private from its inception, though by 1968, with sales an estimated $40 million, profits about $4 million, it was said that financial observers had put a $100 million price tag on the business. (Revson's figures that same year showed sales of $314 million, net profits $31 million.)

Many explanations were proffered about Estée's determination to stay privately held—all in the family, divided equally among Joe, Estée, Leonard, and Ronald. Obviously, keeping the business in the family turned out to be a pragmatic and wise decision. But fundamentally, her need to hold on to it connected with something in her nature, something private, something secretive, something quintessentially Mama and Papa.

Ancky Johnson, Charles Revson's wife for twenty years, before his marriage to Lyn Sheresky, talked about encountering Estée after Revson's death. Ancky and Estée are neighbors in Palm Beach. Estée had heard about Revson's will and she was appalled. Although Revlon had long ago gone public, Charles Revson could have made provisions for his sons to maintain some kind of power within the company; this he had not done. Ancky Johnson said, "Estée told me, 'What was wrong with Charles! He had two children. He worked all his life for the business. Then he *gives it away to strangers.*' She was really upset about it."

Leonard, who would be made president of Lauder in 1972 (Estée then moving up to chairman of the board), turned out to be one of the best justifications for nepotism in the history of any business. He was the man who pushed Lauder into the real big time while retaining the unequivocal respect of his associates and competitors.

According to Tony Liebler, Leonard has "one of the best minds in the business. He tends to live in the shadow, but I think he has the respect of the industry. More so than Estée. Estée is like the Queen of England versus Leonard as Margaret Thatcher."

A man who is one of the company's most threatening competitors contends, "Estée would be nothing if it weren't for Leonard. Leonard is the brains behind that organization. That company would probably be a twenty-five-million-dollar business if it weren't for Leonard. Honest to God, Leonard did it all. I'll give her Youth-Dew. I'll give her gift-with-purchase. I'll give her standing in line to see buyers. [All rather considerable "gives."] But he developed it into a company that is far and away the largest in department stores today."

Estée Lauder had less success with her second launch, Ronald. He was as different from his much older brother as Joe was different from Estée. He is taller than Leonard by an inch or two and is said to resemble neither of his parents. Like Leonard, Ronald attended the highly regarded Bronx High School of Science. He made Arista, headed the General Organization, and served as publicity director of the Biology Club, the Math Bulletin, the Art Committee, and the Forum; the last was a student group that recruited such diverse lecturing luminaries as Eleanor Roosevelt, Norman Thomas, Corliss Lamont, Roy Cohn, and the editors of *MAD* magazine. Like Leonard, he went to the Wharton School at the University of Pennsylvania, but then studied abroad, taking a master's in business in Brussels, studying literature at the Sorbonne. Unlike Leonard, who did not begin to learn French until he was forty, Ronald picked up several languages along the way. He has a fluency in German and French, a smattering of Hungarian, Croatian, and Swedish. A bilingual colleague at Lauder comments, "He probably speaks more languages with an American accent than anyone I know."

Ronald described his apprenticeship in the company to Marilyn Bender. Though he grew up in far more affluent surroundings than Leonard, he spent time at the Lauder plant working under his father. But he recounted that period with a strong aversion. He preferred the period he spent helping launch his family's products in France, living what he termed "the life of Aly Khan for six months."

Ronald Lauder married Jo Carole Knoff in 1967. They have two daughters, Aerin and Jane. Jo Carole, a graduate of Temple University, came from Bloomington, Delaware. He called her "my Early American bride." Both daughters-in-law worked in the Lauder organization, Evelyn with more enthusiasm than Jo Carole. Evelyn is often compared to Estée because of her ambition and her social talents. Jo Carole and Joe Lauder, on the other hand, laughed about their own similarities. She joked with Joe on late nights out, "I know you'd rather be home too."

Estée really wanted it, so Ronald allowed himself to become part of the company. But it was obvious to observers that his heart and his talent lay elsewhere. A longtime friend of the Lauders, who had watched Ronald grow up, joined that family for dinner one night. Her husband began talking about German expressionist painting. She was amazed by the change in Ronald: "I'd never heard him speak more than thirty seconds without somebody shutting him up. Clearly, he had little to say about the business. But when he started talking about *art*, that was something else again. We were amazed by his knowledge."

Nonetheless, Ronald came home to Lauder. At twenty-nine, he was made executive vice-president of Clinique Laboratories, nice for Estée, not so nice for Arthur Noto. Noto had been the business head of Clinique, Carol Phillips the creative force. According to Noto, he had been with the company for three and a half years when Leonard, who'd hired him, came to him one day. "My mother and father want to put Ronald into the job," he said. Noto left to join Erno Laszlo.

It was a strength of Ronald's that he somehow knew his limitations well enough to point to if not to be deterred by them. "Am I as brilliant as my mother or my brother? No," he went on to the obvious delectation of Marilyn Bender. "Am I a child of this environment? Yes. Am I a typical twenty-nine-year-old boy? No. I'm a businessman in my own way. When I come to a store, I won't negotiate. I have the finest products and you should have it, I tell them. It works. When I have a sales meeting in Los Angeles, I have it at dinner at the Bistro. It is very important to me that Clinique be run as sophisticatedly and elegantly, as top notch as possible. My strength is I really enjoy what I'm doing. I run the thing the way it should be done. I'm also the most happy person I know. I'm extraordinarily content. I'm the sweetest guy I know. I love people."

Leonard was, under the best of circumstances, a high-voltage fellow, revved up, on the go, always two or three hours late for dinner with friends because there were things that had to be done. At work, he exhorted his colleagues, "I *want* you nervous. I want you to be nervous. Are you nervous?" One of his executives remembers, "It would *make* you nervous."

79

With Ronald around, Leonard was made even crazier. Estée, who could not keep her hands off Ronald at meetings, would stand up and boast about his increasing sales—this at a time when Ronald was participating in the launch of yet another Lauder satellite, Prescriptives. Ronald had been given two accounts, Bamberger's and John Wanamaker, and each showed greater volume. An ex-Lauder executive recalled Leonard sitting mute but seething: "What was *not* said at those meetings was that for every one dollar they made they were spending four to get it. Ronald put twenty girls behind the counter when they should have had four. And I think there was a certain amount of resentment. It was obvious to everyone that she favored Ronald. And Leonard worked so hard!"

8

QUEEN ESTÉE

With Leonard playing Margaret Thatcher to her Queen Elizabeth, Estée had the freedom to roam, to build, to acquire. And so she did.

Her fear of heights apparently conquered, the company moved to sumptuous quarters at the newly built General Motors Building in 1969. Lauder occupied 123 offices on the thirty-seventh floor and part of the thirty-ninth. Revson was above her, the Revlon organization spreading its 600 people over the top five floors of what came to be known as the General Odors Building.

Revson and Estée took different elevators to their offices, so they managed to avoid meeting on the home front. They were thrown together once when Andrew Goodman of Bergdorf Goodman invited the industry elite to celebrate the refurbishment of his cosmetics department. Harry Doyle was talking to Estée in the penthouse elevator when Revson and coterie entered. And Harry, who worked for Revson, said, "Estée, have you ever met Charles Revson?"

Revson smiled *thin*. And probably would have preferred amenities. As the packed elevator began to ascend, Estée let him have it, shaking her finger at the back of his head.

"One of *your* sales executives wrote a letter about *my* firm. And I have a copy of that letter in my office," she began.

Revson ducked. "We ought to talk about that."

Estée would not be stilled. "I don't want to talk to you," she continued. "You're stealing my people away. You're copying my products . . ."

She and Joe were living by that time in the former Arthur Lehman mansion on East 75th Street in Manhattan. They had moved to a better neighborhood in the south of France, Saint-Jean-Cap-Ferrat, where they usually spent July and August at their Villa Abri. Estée claimed that the air in the south of France inspired the creation of several of her perfumes. Breathing deeply, she told a writer from *W*, "This is how I wanted my eau de toilette for men to smell. It's fresh and herbal."

From the Christmas holidays through March, Estée and Joe were at their twenty-seven-room Palm Beach place. "This is my English home," she explained to a visitor. "This is not a beach house. I want to live here as formally as in New York."

She loved her houses, but appeared not to know *quite* how to live in them. Or at least she didn't live in them the way her burgeoning circle of social friends lived in theirs.

Mary Sanford visited her in Palm Beach one day and Estée showed her around. Mrs. Sanford remembers thinking it odd that Estée didn't have her own quarters.

"Where's *your* bedroom?" Mrs. Sanford inquired.

"I sleep with my husband," Estée Lauder replied.

Nina Schick, a Russian émigrée raised in Paris, owned the Green Thumb Flower Shop on the East Side of New York near Estée's mansion. Mrs. Schick became Estée's florist and floral arranger soon after Estée moved into the house. When she was in New York, Estée entertained every Saturday night. Mrs. Schick would drop by on Saturday morning, usually on her way to a weekend in East Hampton, to leave the flowers and, invariably, chat with her about that evening's arrangements. Estée frequently asked her for suggestions. The table, Nina Schick thought, was always overdone, *groaning* with the weight of Estée's possessions. Mrs. Schick remembers, "She wanted to take *all* her silver out and put it on the table. I always wanted to tell her, 'It's *not* a store. Put it away. People *know* that you have it.' "

The florist was especially oppressed by the fact that the house was always overheated, dark. Shades were drawn. She recalls only one live-in servant, although Estée hired droves, including footmen in white gloves, for the dinner itself: "It was as if the house was only open for when the guests came."

There were times when Estée could be difficult to deal with. Once she was very displeased with the choice of flowers Mrs. Schick had made; Mrs. Schick defended her merchandise. And Estée countered, "Maybe they're *good* enough for your *East Hampton friends*, but they're not good enough for me."

Estée was climbing with a great deal of success. In the south of France she befriended Mrs. Florence J. Gould, the daughter-in-law of railroad magnate Jay Gould. She was an enormously wealthy, hard-drinking, art-collecting heiress. On account of Estée's friendship with Mrs. Gould—who had moved, according to one art collector "from paintings by pathetic Bernard Buffet" to a great collection that included a Van Gogh landscape, which would eventually sell for $9.9 million, and a considerable group of Bonnards—Tom Hoving allowed Estée to have the very first private party ever at the Metropolitan Museum of Art for Mrs. Gould, whose collection he was interested in acquiring. Attending were Betsy Bloomingdale, Mrs. T. Suffern Tailer, Nan Kempner, and, of course, Mrs. Gould, who wore Yves Saint Laurent. Estée was in blue Givenchy and sapphires.

Estée had also befriended the Begum Aga Khan, whom she met in the south of France. The Begum, an ex-French beauty queen, was the wife of the Aga Khan, spiritual leader of the Ismaili Moslem sect. A friend who goes back with Estée to the late fifties remembers one night in the early seventies when he, his wife, Joe, and Estée were chatting in Monte Carlo, all of them attending a ball that was being given by Earl Blackwell. They were walking down the steps that led to the sea when Estée picked up peripherally the sight of flashbulbs popping. He remembers Estée reacting instantly: "She looked down and she said, 'Oh my God, it's the Begum.' She picked up her skirt to her knees and ran—not a spring chicken by this time, OK?—ran down the steps to be sure she was photographed with the Begum Aga Khan."

The Duchess of Windsor continued to head Estée's list; she was forever running off to see and be seen with the Windsors and, for a time after the Duke's death, with the Duchess. When a movie documentary about the Duke opened in New York in 1972, she was at a private party given for the couple at Bergdorf Goodman. (Rose Kennedy approached her and introduced Estée to Ted Kennedy. "I want you to meet the lady who keeps me beautiful," Mrs. Kennedy said, to which her son replied, "Mother, I didn't know you needed anyone to keep you beautiful.") The Shiny Sheet in Palm Beach was kept dutifully apprised of all Estée's appointments with the pair. "Mr. and Mrs. Joseph Lauder leave for New York to dine with the Duke and Duchess of Windsor before traveling on to Europe. The couple will return to Palm Beach within two weeks to host a special dinner for the Duke and Duchess." . . . "Estée Lauder will hostess her kind of party for three hundred at Maxim's the night after she dines with the Duchess of Windsor."

In an unusually frank and lucid interview with the Shiny Sheet in 1969, Estée told Marian Christy, in a column called "After a Fashion": "Many people try to use me, my power, my influence, my money. My truest friends are the ones who don't expect anything from me. The only thing they want is the pleasure of my company."

She then went on to name her most-trusted friends, her "inner circle": the Begum Aga Khan, the Duchess of Windsor, and millionairess Mrs. Frank J. Gould.

Estée, 1980. (*Dustin Pittman*/Women's Wear Daily)

Estée Lauder and Princess Grace. (*Tony Palmieri*/Women's Wear Daily)

Estée Lauder with Rose Kennedy and Ambassador Guilford Dudley.

Carol Phillips, president of Clinique.

(*Tony Palmieri* / Women's Wear Daily)

Estée and Joe Lauder with Mrs. T. Suffern Tailer.

Estée and the Duchess of Windsor at West Palm Beach railroad station.

Estée and the Duke of
Windsor at West Palm
Beach railroad station.

The Duke and Duchess of Windsor leaving West Palm Beach.

Estée and Joe Lauder with Helen Gurley Brown. (*Irv Steinberg/Globe Photos*)

Left: C. Z. and Winston Guest with Estée (and unidentified woman). (*Dustin Pittman/Women's Wear Daily*)   *Right:* Estée in Central Park playground. (*New York* Daily News)

Estée and Joe Lauder at the opening of the Ancient Play Garden in Central Park, which the Lauders funded. (*AP/Wide World Photos*)

Estée Lauder at Cap Ferrat, south of France. (*Guy Marineau*/Women's Wear Daily)

Estée and Joseph Lauder shortly before Joe's death. (*Cathy Blaivas*/Women's Wear Daily)

Estée began giving rather famous parties in the seventies, the most celebrated being her annual George Washington's Day Birthday Party. Estée's fetes were black-tie affairs held on the tremendous lawn that extended to her sea wall. She erected a tent. Hired Neil Smith's orchestra. And had the two Cuban caterers standing at the door dressed up as George and Martha Washington.

Hostesses in Palm Beach, of course, outdid themselves to party creatively; Estée was no exception. Her invitations were each hand-delivered. One of the recipients remembers receiving his: "It looked like you were getting a very expensive watch from Cartier's. You started opening it. Underneath the brown paper was red-coated paper, very bright. And inside was a betel-nut box, and inside the betel-nut box was an invitation *and* a chocolate-covered cherry."

They were delivered around ten-thirty, when "the girls" generally awake and begin telephoning each other. On this particular morning, the bon mot was the bon-bon: "Did you get Estée's cherry?" one Palm Beach hostess asked another.

Then she gave a series of parties for twenty-four on three consecutive nights. Identical parties, with the same menu, the same decor, and the same flowers. That kind of behavior inevitably nettled a lot of people because she was obviously dividing her friends into Group A, Group B, and Group C. A veteran observer of the social scene in Palm Beach maintained, "She'd have a party with C. Z. Guest and that group, and the next night, with the same flowers, she'd have her Jewish friends."

Estée perforce offended a lot of people, including a steely, equally ambitious, equally brazen social type who began giving serial parties herself. Estée telephoned around town and determined, much to her dismay, that she had been invited to the B party. Thereupon, she called the hostess to say look here, why am I in your B group and not in your A group; to which the hostess replied that Estée was not going to be in her A group because she'd been in Estée's B group. "Why should I invite you to my A party when you invite me to your B?"

There ensued, presumably, a détente.

There were some fences, however, that were not so easily mended. Her old friend Jo Copeland reportedly expressed resentment, as a Jew and as an old friend. Another old acquaintance has not forgotten meeting Estée at a fashion function at the Metropolitan Museum. "She was standing with some princess and I walked over to say hello, and she kind of motioned me away with a slight pushing motion with her hand. In other words, bug off. Estée Lauder lost many of the people she knew and loved on her way up."

Socialite Pauline Ney maintained that Estée had been, early on, "nice and quiet at parties. And then later on I changed my opinion of her. She started saying, 'And I said to the Duchess and the Duchess said to me.'"

Estée's social success did nothing to abate her constant-verging-on-comical reluctance to disclose her background, including her Jewishness. Seemingly nothing was known about the Rosenthals, and virtually nothing about her sister Renée. However, a man named Larry Borston, who had managed the only hotel in Palm Beach to serve kosher food, remembers that Estée's sister stayed there, that Estée spent time with her, that the sister seemed much older though she was in fact only two years older, and that she was quiet, unprepossessing, and not well.

Though she kept her sister in the private part of her life, Estée had no hesitation in introducing a Catholic nun in full habit around the resort community (and in the office), as a relative—which she probably was, according to a member of the family who remembers that there was in fact a cousin who converted to Catholicism and took vows.

The irony is, of course, that everybody knew Estée was Jewish, and those who came to know and like her were simply and somewhat fondly amused by the elaborate charade.

Among those not amused were the denizens of the old-guard Everglades Club, where there was an understanding about Jews. A member explained that if you are Jewish you may only attend a function in a specific room rented by a member for a specific occasion: "You can't just take [Jewish] people for dinner or lunch. You cannot just take [Jewish] people into the dining room. When I go down there—and I have a guest membership— it's very upsetting to me because I cannot invite any Jewish friends to lunch or dinner."

The Palm Beach Everglades Club is notorious for not admitting Jews. As recently as April 1985, a former director of the club, who was once the United States Ambassador to Pakistan, told *The Miami Herald* airily, "If there is such a rule, what's wrong with it? It wouldn't be a private club if anybody could be brought into it."

The previous month, in March 1985, a cocktail party planned at the Everglades by the supporters of the New York City Ballet was canceled when the ballet directors learned that the function was to be held at the Everglades, claiming the club practiced "exclusionary policy." Robert Terry, a member of the Everglades board of directors, responded, "It's a private club. We make our own rules and regulations at the club."

Sometime in the mid-seventies C. Z. Guest broke the rule when she took Estée and a group of other friends to the general, gentile space for lunch. During the course of the repast, Estée was spotted by an irate member who telephoned an executive of the club. He appeared immediately and passed Mrs. Guest a note: "You are out of order." C. Z., an avid sportswoman, was reprimanded and punished. She lost her tennis privileges for a time.

Estée telephoned Mary Sanford the next morning "horrified"

that Mrs. Guest had been reprimanded for bringing her. Mary Sanford gasped, "Estée, whatever possessed you?"

Estée replied, "I thought it would be all right because C. Z. took me."

The Everglades episode has become folklore in Palm Beach. People still talk about it. Everybody knows it happened. Agnes Ash, the editor of the Shiny Sheet, maintains it happened before she arrived on the scene in 1977. "C. Z. told me about it," she said. "She was infuriated. And Winston was mad at C. Z. for causing the fuss."

It is said that both James Brady, then of *Women's Wear Daily* and Charlotte Curtis of *The New York Times* chronicled the episode. Brady remains unable to find his story. Curtis corresponds on April 12, 1985: "I'm afraid I cannot help. I wasn't there. I do not remember when it happened. I did not write about it. But no matter what anyone tells you, there was a great fuss and to-do, but Mrs. Guest was more nearly severely reprimanded than suspended, and she [Mrs. Guest] screamed to high heaven. The Everglades Club is another matter. It is stuffy, stodgy and highly selective. . . ."

On February 10, 1984, Suzanne Garment of *The Wall Street Journal* ran a blind item about the incident: "One very prominent socialite brought a Jewish cosmetics queen to lunch and got a reprimand."

The Miami Herald finally pursued the story more than a year later. But Estée remains unable to make any sense of the situation, which provoked in her not rage but a kind of screwy incredulity. It's as though the episode is *still* not clear to her. She talked to *The Miami Herald* in 1985, and the *Herald* reported: "In an interview last month, Estée Lauder, whose father is Jewish, confirmed that the article [a blind item in *The Wall Street Journal*] referred to a luncheon she attended with three or four other women. C. Z. Guest was the hostess.

" 'She got in trouble, but not for [taking] me,' Estée said, suggesting that Guest's lunch group was simply too large. 'It wasn't because they were Jewish. I don't know what it was . . .' "

Estée is probably as baffled as she is baffling where her background and her Jewish ethnicity are concerned. There is doubtless great division and guilt and self-loathing. Her WASP fantasies, so successfully utilized in the creation of the whole Lauder look, were not always stronger than the habits and rites associated with her deep Jewish roots.

She privately observes, for instance, the traditions of Passover. Ira Levy went to Palm Beach one Passover season to show her the Lauder Christmas line he had designed. Estée met him at the mansion door wearing a hoover apron and a *schmata* on her head. She was in the middle of cleansing the ocean-front house of *chometz* (whatever is not kosher for Passover)—a ritual harkening back and signifying a new beginning for the Jewish people after their liberation from Egypt.

She will sit down with a Jewish seamstress and boast of doing her own cooking for the holidays. Among her Jewish friends, she has been known to speak fluent Yiddish. "*Kuk im on!*" (Just look at him), she bubbled to a Jewish companion, lovingly gazing at her husband Joe.

An ex-employee of Helena Rubinstein who socialized a great deal with Estée observes, "When she turns on the charm, there's no one more charming than Estée. She's done everything possible to clean up her act. But underneath it all, she's really a Jewish mama, a typical, lower-middle-class Jewish lady, and she deserves tremendous credit for building that business."

Joe Lauder tagged along to Estée's social functions with loving dedication and a soothing glass of scotch in his hand. Once, after weeks of back-to-back Palm Beach parties, he telephoned Leonard in New York, hoping for a reason to get out of there.

"Don't you have any problems in New York?" he pleaded.

"No, Dad," Leonard said, "everything's just fine."

Though everybody liked Joe, he seemed to have no special men friends in Palm Beach. Those friends he did have were old New York friends, not especially successful. He kibitzed with a photographer whom he especially liked. "How you doing, *Bubele?* What a drag. I wish I were home so I could take my shoes off. Same old faces."

At parties, Estée fussed over him, prepared his plates, and monitored his drinking.

Harry Doyle was with her and Joe one night at the Celebrity Room in Palm Beach. Ted Straeter's band was playing, and Harry asked her to dance. She said, "No, Joe gets very jealous." Finally, she agreed.

He remembers that she was not easy to lead. "She's a big woman and I tried to dance her around the room, but I wasn't able to make her turn. She was keeping *my* back to the important tables so that she could wave at everybody. And she's saying in my ear, 'Harry, let me tell you how I developed Youth-Dew.' I said, 'Oh, shit, Estée.' She said, 'Don't talk like that!' "

9

LISTEN TO
YOUR CUSTOMERS

Leonard Lauder addressed a group of professional women called AWED (American Woman's Economic Development) in 1985 and outlined the strengths of Estée Lauder, Inc. It was a ten-point address, delivered affably in his reedy and somewhat regionally dentalized speaking voice, fluent and free of his former stammer. The bulwark of the recounted success story was: Listen to your mother, listen to your customer, understand the essential nature of your business. "Stick to it," he advised, "if you're good in something, stay in what you're good at."

What the Lauders were good at, from the very inception of the business, was the care and cosseting of their customers where they bought their product: point of purchase, the store. Allan Mottus, a cogent and intelligent writer and consultant on the cosmetics scene, commented that the Lauders were less producers of cosmetics than preeminent merchandisers.

Estée possessed an understanding of her customer that was almost preternatural; Leonard learned that and then some. This emphasis on what happens at the counter is called "sell-thru." It is the flip side of "sell-in," which is more or less what Revson did and what Revlon continues to do. "Sell-in" means create a demand (advertise), get the goods out, and sell them to a customer whose appetite is already whetted when she comes in off the street. The Lauders had always understood that sell-thru created a vacuum for sell-in.

Sell-thru is expensive; so is dealing with big, important department stores who own the "real estate" (trade talk for the kind and quality of space each company is allotted by the stores). Suppliers clamor for space in Bloomingdale's New York store, for instance, where over half of the main floor is devoted to cosmetics. Stores can and do exert considerable leverage where promotion, sales help, and advertising campaigns are concerned.

Frank Shields, whilom executive at Revlon and Rubinstein, bitterly told *Forbes* magazine in 1982, "The stores stick it to cosmetics manufacturers every way they can." He cited the fact that they often billed manufacturers at full-rate for so-called cooperative advertising (they may not pass along the discounted prices newspapers charge their big retail advertisers; some manufacturers may have to pay, say, $7,000 for a seven-column advertisement, even though Bendel's name runs along the bottom of the page). These and other unreasonable demands can be made.

In Manhattan, for instance, companies must pay the freight for cooperative advertising, an onerous demand on a smaller company. Why? According to Harry Doyle of Revlon, "The stores demand it. You go to Bloomingdale's and they say you pay one hundred percent. And you say, 'Hell, I don't have it. I'm a starving business.' And they say 'too bad.' "

In the old days—when Lauder was a sixteen-million-dollar company—it was even costlier proportionately to deal with the big, prestigious store. According to Tony Liebler, the company was compelled to support its department-store habit with a subsidiary line of fine speciality stores throughout the country. They would *permit* a small, quality store in Athens, Georgia, or Mount Kisco, New York, or Cheyenne, Wyoming, to sell their line if they met certain standards. Liebler recalled that somebody would have to check out the store to look for signs: Did they sell Russell Stover candy, for instance? These stores were easy to service and lucrative. After the initial visit—something like a social worker calling on a prospective set of adoptive parents—the specialty stores were easy to service. "And the reason the stores wanted Estée Lauder," says Liebler, "is because they saw forty feet of Lauder at Saks and because of the prestige advertising."

As Lauder grew, the shoe moved over. Having built up a business cooperatively with the department stores, Estée behaved with proprietorship. A Neiman-Marcus executive who watched her in action in the late sixties recalled, "She'd come into the stores and almost *shove* Charles of the Ritz on the floor and go *storming* upstairs if she found that she had lost one inch of real estate. She'd threaten to pull the whole line out if anything was out of order."

Neiman's, the executive said, needed Estée. "The Arden company was still going but losing its impact. Revlon was mass-merchandised, so we didn't carry it. We used to give her a lot of advantages as to advertising, as to paying for salespeople. It was a mutual thing. And we built a helluva business together, but God forbid if . . . Her local detail people came in shivering and sweating for fear that she'd find something wrong. If her local people weren't doing a job, and she was the first to hire detail people that actually lived in the area, she'd show up herself. I rue the day that she got over her fear of flying."

The dynamics changed according to bottom lines, state and federal laws, store policies, clout, and cacophony. The boss of Neiman-Marcus, Stanley Marcus, who is himself an entrepreneur of some character, made it a policy not to allow the people in *his* stores to work for Lauder or any other cosmetics company. The former Neiman executive, who worked under Stanley Marcus, remembered, "We were powerful enough in that sense to get away with it, but many of the other stores in the country have Lauder salespeople, and they're paid by Lauder, and they won't look at anyone else."

Even though Marcus forbade the direct use of Lauder personnel on his premises, there were ways to finesse, to buy the loyalty of salespeople without actually signing their checks. There is something called salary charge-back. Under the Saks plan, manufacturers pay a percentage of shipments; they get a check back for $16\frac{2}{3}$ percent of net shipments; that goes toward the salary of salespeople and also toward commissions. There was also something, less formally structured, called the Estée plan. If she discovered that a Laszlo person was selling a larger volume than a Lauder person, she would demand that the Laszlo person be moved over to the Lauder counter.

Estée was aware and Neiman-Marcus was aware of what her line had come to mean to them, especially after Lord & Taylor and Saks came to Texas; Neiman's had no alternative but to give more and more leverage in return for certain exclusivities. She would barge into board meetings and instruct the executives on the care and handling of her line. When all else failed, she would telephone Stanley Marcus to say, "You've forgotten who your friends are."

"When I was with Neiman's in the North Park store," the executive recounted, "we were doing about twelve million in cosmetics, and I bet you six million of it was Lauder. She was doing fifteen percent of the store's volume, and that's a lot of volume. The prospect of her removing her line was a deadly one. We were exclusive in all of North Texas, except for Frost Brothers."

She was a tyrant, but a creative one. Among her many in-store innovations was the outpost boutique—the little niche in the sportswear department for the *sportive* Lauder product. She thought it up, demanded the emplacement, and everybody profited.

When the day-to-day operations of the business passed gradually to Leonard, the emphasis on sell-thru did not change. What he did, however, was to professionalize their preeminence as merchandisers. Instead of using tantrums and old loyalties and store raids, Leonard began in a systematic and coordinated way to plan ahead with the various stores. Stores guaranteed in writing a year in advance the kind and quantity of merchandise they would buy, their level of advertising, the quality and quantity of real estate; in turn Lauder would promise exclusives, in-store promotions, larger payments to sales personnel.

Richard Salomon, who headed Charles of the Ritz until it went woefully public and who is the nephew of that company's founder, credits Leonard's planning mechanisms with the spectacular growth of the company. "Leonard's planning is what made the business what it is today," Salomon says. "His planning mechanism is responsible for the real success of that business. He created that—not Charles Revson, not I, not Estée. He would sit down with store heads, set a goal for the year, and plan how it was that they would reach that goal. It was reduced to writing. It wasn't a legal contract, but an understanding of what would govern next year's operations. . . . Stores were impressed not only by the method but by the volume achieved, and by the fact that they consistently reached these increased goals."

The company had always been exceedingly closed-mouthed about the role of Estée versus Leonard. It is one of the aspects of the business they are most resistant to defining. There was never any doubt about Joe; he was always at the plant in Melville overseeing operations. There was never any doubt about Ronald; he was taking Italian lessons and using the company as a kind of holding operation until he was ready for something bigger. There was never any doubt that Leonard was there on an almost day-to-day basis and that Estée was away a lot, promoting Estée Lauder, Inc., by promoting Estée Lauder. But as to who had what kind of authority—that was the most difficult question to get answered.

Typically, the most precise information came from Marilyn Bender in 1973. As to choice of products, Leonard told Bender,

"We will defer to Mrs. Lauder's ultimate decision. I can blithely spend millions on a certain investment without asking anyone, but I wouldn't launch a body lotion that contains fragrance without her signed approval."

Estée's hegemony in the fragrance end of the company is undisputed. Just as Charles Revson was "the eye," Estée remained "the nose." No matter that IFF actually made the "juice," her status as olfactory honcho at Estée Lauder cannot be gainsaid.

Allan Mottus remembers when her fragrance, Private Collection, was about to debut. He was in his office one morning when Saks telephoned. The Lauder people had just taken back the first shipment of the fragrance, which was to be launched momentarily. Had she taken it back from Saks to give it instead to Bergdorf? Mottus telephoned Bergdorf; their stock had just gone out the door too. Mottus rang up "one of the right people" at Lauder. "Everyone is calling me about this launch," he said. "What's wrong?"

An incredulous executive at Lauder told Allan that Mrs. Lauder had insisted on the recall because the fragrance was missing one ingredient.

Allan Mottus says, "It didn't have 'dunk-dunk' in it. They told her at the company, 'Nobody will *know* the difference.' And Mrs. Lauder said, 'But *I'll* know the difference!' Charles [Revson] would have done the same thing. With all the other companies, the perfumers can get away with murder. With Mrs. Lauder, what *she* wants is what she gets."

She has an especially passionate and proprietary feeling about fragrance. Listen to her company hagiographers in their press release entitled ESTÉE LAUDER; PERFUMER TO THE PACE-SETTERS OF TODAY AND TOMORROW:

What is the story behind Estée Lauder's phenomenal success in the perfume world?

"I am a woman," states Lauder simply, "I love perfume. I wear it myself. Always. So I know what a woman wants in a perfume."

Actually there is more to the story than she modestly admits. Estée Lauder is the only woman directly involved in both creating and marketing important prestige fragrances. Her interest is not only personal. It is passionate.

"Wearing perfume is like loving," Estée Lauder continues. "You can't be stingy: You must give yourself to it freely—abundantly. Not a little here and there.

"Creating a fragrance is something like composing a symphony. You play notes against each other, drawing from the chemist's battery of all possible scents. Some sweet. Some low. Others pungent. Or mysterious."

After the mysteries of the creative process come the all-important testing. Estée Lauder tests and tries and re-tests every formula. On herself. On her friends. Everywhere she goes. . . .

If we would name names, you'd be surprised at the famous ladies, including a Duchess or two and a well-known princess [who undoubtedly was most grateful for Estée's annual donation to the Red Cross of Monaco] who make up Estée Lauder's "testing panel." Plus one celebrated beauty who swears she wouldn't be caught on or off the best-dressed list unless she's wearing a perfume personally created by Estée Lauder! . . .

"When I ask someone to try a new scent, there must be an instant reaction. *'Great!'* or *'Impossible!'* Then I know I'm on the right track. If the scent evokes only a lukewarm reaction, I throw the formula away. Successful fragrances must stir emotions. If it's truly a great one, people either love it or hate it. Nothing in between! . . ."

In the woman's field, since Youth-Dew in 1954, she had introduced other fragrances: Estée, 1968; Azurée, 1969; Aliage, 1972; Private Collection, 1973 (finally with 'dunk-dunk'); Estée Daytime and Eau d'Aliage, 1976. For Aliage, which she called her "sports perfume," she even posed for the Shiny Sheet, dressed in tennis whites, holding her racket like a salad fork. The copy read, "Walking off her private court at the Lauder's South Ocean Boulevard home, perspiration dampened both her hair and her triumph. It set her to wondering about preserving a woman's feminity during strenuous physical exercise."

" 'I started to think,' she confided to writer Marth Parrish,

97

'you don't wear a flowered hat to go bicycle riding . . . why would you wear a flower perfume?' "

All of her fragrances made enough money to keep her in tennis whites, but none of them finally had the dazzle or the impact of the original Youth-Dew.

Meanwhile, the dazzle and impact of American fragrances like Youth-Dew and Revson's Charlie (1973) had helped to reverse the trend away from subtle French to life-style American scents. This had put the French in an innovative state of mind. Or at least prepared them for one of the basic cyclical reversals that are endemic to all aspects of the fashion industry. The besieged French houses began to plan for a reaction, a return to the *haute gamme*, or pricey, category. But with a difference. They searched for a hybrid, with the cachet of a French designer's name and the impact and endurance of an American "juice."

Such a hybrid was Opium, whose creation involved the talented and world-famous designer, Yves Saint Laurent.

Opium, it was claimed, emerged conceptually when Saint Laurent began to think Middle Eastern in 1975 as the theme of a fashion collection. He conceived of a perfume package—dramatically lacquered orange, a long black tassle that might be worn as a pendant, a flacon designed to look like the containers in which opium had been shipped to the Orient in 1800—and primarily the name *Opium*, with all the languor and sensuality that the drug conjured up. The juice was done by Rouré Bertrand DuPont, one of IFF's big competitors, drawing on oriental notes.

Launched in Paris in 1977, the fragrance was hugely successful. And it had the name and the look of a great French designer.

Amelia Bassin, a consultant in the field of fragrance, who accepts as a given that imitation is not only the highest form of flattery but an expected and common occurrence in the industry, chuckles, "I remember when Opium first came out. Opium was a kind of knock-off of Youth-Dew, which was smart. But they livened it with some very sparkling spice notes, so that it wasn't quite as sweet and heavy as Youth-Dew. It opened in Paris and it was a *sensation*—everybody was talking about it . . . About the same time, Estée Lauder was planning to introduce a version of Youth-Dew, which I assume was going to be a much lighter version. *Then* she announced that she was coming out with Cinnabar. And in about six weeks they really put that line together. They must have put some pressure on their suppliers. Cinnabar was very much like Opium, the color of the box and the tassles. She did it so fast that many of the bottles, which take a long time to make, still said 'Soft Youth-Dew.' Opium has been a greater success."

With all their talk about quality, patience, and prudence, the Cinnabar response proved that the company, when challenged, was perfectly capable of flying by the seat of its pants—willy-nilly, piggy-to-market. With all their Leonard Lauder-induced planning mechanisms, the company was still basically entrepreneurial in a pinch. Mama came home for this one! Like Charles Revson before her, she could not concede that anyone else had a basic and fairly inalienable right to market a competitive product.

Finally unclear in the Cinnabar-Opium fragrance war was what it was that Estée put into her flacons, some of which were and some of which were not labeled Youth-Dew—all of which she called Cinnabar. What came through loud and clear was her *outrage*. She told *Women's Wear Daily* in September 1978, "When I saw Opium, I almost passed out. If Yves Saint Laurent knew about fragrance and my Youth-Dew, he would have never done Opium. Opium is my Youth-Dew but with a tassel."

Opium experienced certain difficulties on account of its name. The Australian government refused importation, claiming the name misrepresented the product. There was a great outcry from the Chinese-American community, a spokesman for which complained that the blithe and playful commercial references to a drug that had done such terrible damage to the Chinese people was reprehensible, as offensive to Chinese citizens as naming a fragrance Holocaust might be to the Jews. Phoenix House, a drug rehabilitation center, objected and so did *Advertising Age*. E. R. Squibb, the conservative pharmaceutical house that had acquired Charles of the Ritz, which was distributing Opium in the United States, attempted to convince Saint Laurent to change the name; he demurred. The Opium launch went, more or less, according to schedule, although Martin H. Schmidt, Ritz group vice-president, contended that the schedule had been revamped when they discovered, early in 1978, "that Lauder was in the process of trying to knock us off . . . So Opium came out that fall, instead of 1979, as originally planned."

In the fall of 1978, Opium threw an incredibly expensive press-celebrity party aboard a tall ship, the *Peking*, which sailed Manhattan's East River carrying a thousand-pound Buddha, white cattleya orchids from Hawaii, twenty pounds of red sturgeon, fifty orders of Peking Duck, strawberries, champagne, and Truman Capote.

Opium "opened" at Saks and Bloomingdale's simultaneously. That her own favorite launching pad, Saks Fifth Avenue, had taken Opium instead of Cinnabar must have been grievously offensive to Estée. Equally devastating was the assessment of Margaret Hayes, vice-president and divisional manager of cosmetics at Saks, who told Enid Nemy of *The New York Times* that the Opium debut was "the most successful launching I've come in contact with." Mike Blumenfeld of Bloomingdale's, agreed that it was the "biggest introduction of a perfume we've ever had."

Cinnabar debuted at Lord & Taylor. Allan Mottus wrote in *Product Marketing* in November 1978 that though Lord & Taylor was not the premiere launch store one would have expected, Lauder had proven itself, once again, a premiere merchandiser.

He wrote about the models hired by Lauder who stood in black velvet dresses at the store handing out counter cards "just in case anyone short of being blind could possibly miss the Cinnabar displays that dominated the store's entrance. Other models were filling samples from island display areas within the store's broad cosmetic aisles. It was a tour de force even within the realm of extravagant sales promotion."

Cinnabar also featured a pendant, was also oriental in motif, and it was half the price of Saint Laurent's Opium: fifty dollars for an ounce as opposed to one hundred dollars. The crowd at Lord & Taylor also got free samples, lectures from line girls about how Cinnabar was better and much cheaper than Opium, and a glance at Estée Lauder herself, making one of her not-so-rare personal appearances.

Using pressure that an executive at Neiman-Marcus described as "unbelievable," Estée beat Opium to the punch at the prestigious Texas store, which was slated originally to be an Opium launch site. The Cinnabar debut was sandwiched in, according to one trade publication, two weeks before the Opium premiere, much to the dismay of the Guy Laroche people who thought they had the floor exclusively for one of their new scents. *Cosmetic World* reported that "the basic Lauder assault team used every ounce of muscle to jump the gun with its Cinnabar promotion."

Both fragrances did quite well, being as difficult to ignore as Lindbergh in the sky, and this despite a newspaper strike, a testament to the viability of the sell-thru push of each producer. But the trade writers were forced to become veritable exegetes, attempting to figure out what it was that Estée Lauder had actually put in the bottle and just when she decided to put it there.

The various histories offered by the Lauder family were not terribly helpful. In September of 1978, just as the tall ship *Peking* was navigating the East River, Estée announced to the press that she had begun working on this spicy exotic fragrance called

Cinnabar two summers before, when she met with IFF representatives in the south of France.

However, prior to that revelation, Ronald Lauder, who was then vice-president of marketing and sales, had described the Cinnabar entity as a selection of "Youth-Dew products repackaged for Christmas"—a selection inspired by Mrs. Lauder's new-found interest in "Chinese lacquer shades of brick red that caps, boxes, and wraps every item in the Cinnabar collection."

So Cinnabar was to have been a look?

That was, more or less, how Margaret Hayes of Saks understood it. She told *Women's Wear Daily* that she "had not been apprised that the collection included a new fragrance. She understood it to be a merchandising technique."

Soft Youth-Dew with red tops?

When informed by *Women's Wear* that Cinnabar was not just a new look but a new and retitled version of Youth-Dew, the industry-savvy Hayes responded, "Based on the price points, I would say Cinnabar is a thrust by a very competitive company with a more broad-based appeal."

Opium for half the price?

Ronald then came back to *Women's Wear*, attempting to elucidate. He said that it had been decided a week earlier that "Cinnabar Soft Youth-Dew would have a fragrance of its own—distinct from classic Youth-Dew and the light version, Soft Youth-Dew." (This was an apparent admission that Estée had altered, at the last minute, the actual perfume to better compete with Opium's phenomenal acceptance.) "Mrs. Lauder," he reported, "decided that Cinnabar Soft Youth-Dew had to be spicier, more oriental." "Cinnabar," he went on, "is not a full-fledged fragrance launch, but it's new. It's Soft Youth-Dew with a twist." Estée herself was reported in *WWD* to have asserted that this new contemporary version of Youth-Dew "in no way indicated that she was displeased with Soft Youth-Dew"; they intended to market each through Christmas and then decide "which way to go."

102

Two fragrances waiting for a bottom line?

The befuddled *Women's Wear* writer, Joan Harting, got back to Ronald Lauder, wondering whether he didn't "see a potential for confusion among Soft Youth-Dew consumers?"

Ronald said that he had put the problem to Estée Lauder and that she had responded, " 'Better a little confusion for the customers and a great product on the counter.' "

And so, in every regard and faithfully, were the admonitions elaborated by Leonard Lauder in his ten-point success program reflected in the Cinnabar launching of 1978: Listen to your mother. Listen to your customer. And stick to what you're good at.

10

POUR L'HOMME

The signally elegant Lauder woman was an *unqualified* success by 1978. She was the incarnation of the company to the customers. Estée had with stunning taste and instinct won them over to her fragrances and cosmetics. The Lauder woman was the projection of the Estée Lauder company—everything about the company, from products to corporate sensibilities, to the show at the counter, to its founder's style of living. She signified the easeful fantasy on behalf of which Josephine Esther Mentzer had dedicated seventy years of her life.

The then current apotheosis of that look was Karen Graham. She had begun posing exclusively for Estée Lauder in 1971. Green-eyed and quite exquisite to look at, she was twenty-five when she agreed to work exclusively for Lauder, thereby forgoing her other top modeling opportunities.

The company, typically, tried to keep Graham under wraps so that she might be perceived neat and pristine. She was, in fact, married to Del Coleman, the head man at Las Vegas's Stardust Hotel. She had married Coleman just as she was about to become Mrs. David Frost; Coleman flew to London at the eleventh hour bearing gifts. "He gave her a big diamond," fashion designer Mollie Parnis said.

Her earnings, too, were a state secret. By 1980 she was making half a million dollars for thirty-five shooting days a year. Good money, but less than the other models who were signed exclusively with other companies: Cheryl Tiegs for Cover Girl, Cristina Ferrare for Bristol-Meyers, and Lauren Hutton for Revlon.

Graham was remarkably perfect, especially in the Lauder fragrance ads: sporty, with glasses perched atop her head, climbing among rare books for "the daylight version of the famous Estée fragrance"; more frequently house- or property-bound (but oh, what houses and property) alone among her extraordinary objets d'art. There was an occasional borzoi, and once or twice a horse.

She appeared only in leading fashion magazines and other publications of distinction: *The New Yorker*, *Town and Country*. Mass-circulation periodicals like *Family Circle* were eschewed. The ostensible reason was given by June Leaman, senior vice-president of creative marketing for Estée Lauder. "First off," she said, "we can't afford to talk specifically to the woman who reads a magazine like that because the circulation is wasteful to us. Too many of their readers are located in areas where they have no access to our products. Secondly, editorial climate is a key factor. A woman reading about beauty and fashion in *Glamour*, for example, is in the mood for us."

Her second rationale was, of course, more candid. She was talking fantasy; she was indicating snob appeal.

The Lauder woman, by way of Karen Graham, was pitching fragrances for women. But Lauder had a subsidiary called Aramis, the men's line, that had grown rather quietly apace since its creation in the sixties. Now, in the late seventies, there appeared to be room for more serious expansion.

There were, however, problems. The selling of men's fragrance was—and continues to be—a delicate business. The imputation of homosexuality looms. No one for a moment would have assumed Karen Graham to be without a husband or a lover of the proper sex, because she always appeared alone in the advertisements. Not so with a male counterpart. There was the complex question of who bought men's fragrances. He wore it, of course.

But who purchased it? Back in 1978 a Lauder executive contended that 70 percent of the time she bought it *for* him! While that was a habit to be encouraged, men, at the same time, needed to be primed and educated and eased up enough to walk comfortably into a department store if the market was to open up beyond the three or four gift-giving occasions of the year.

All of these factors, as well as the lack of tradition and the awfully fragile parameters of masculinity, made the selling and advertising of male fragrance a problem of some consequence.

By 1978 the Lauder organization had a valuable group of men's lines to protect. Aramis, which had been introduced in 1964 as an after-shave and cologne, now constituted more than forty products. Aramis 900, previewed in 1970, with an emphasis on scientific formulation, was thriving. And Estée had high hopes for her newborn Devin, the sporty cologne she claimed was inspired by a recent trip made to the horse country of Lexington, Kentucky. (It was more likely inspired by the introduction of Polo, created by Ralph Lauren and ex-Aramis chief George Friedman.) These various men's lines—all coming under the Aramis umbrella in a way that made the Austro-Hungarian Empire seem well defined—spun off hair sprays, bath soaks, shaving products, deodorants, and all varieties of fragrance, from hardly-there aftershaves to lustier colognes. There was even soap on a rope.

The Aramis subsidiary was, by 1978, selling at an estimated $40 million annually; this compared to about $175 million for the Estée Lauder division and $80 million for Clinique. However, the Aramis products were growing at a robust 18 percent a year, and that appeared to be just the beginning of a healthy trend in the men's fragrance market.

Hazel Bishop, the woman who had become a household word with her formulation of long-lasting lipstick some years before, was now an industry consultant for Evans & Co. in New York.

She wrote that the two most popular Aramis products, after-shave and cologne, accounted for as much as 50 to 80 percent of sales in the men's fragrance category in some department stores; she attributed their popularity to strong masculine appeal, good packaging, good and long-lasting fragrance, status pricing, and clever distribution.

In the December 1977 issue of the trade publication *Soap/Cosmetics/Chemical Specialties*, Bishop predicted that the market would continue to boom. She cited various contributing factors: "more disposable income in the hands of black and Hispanic people who have never been influenced by Anglo-Saxon taboos about the use of male fragrances; more money in the hands of teenagers who found fragrance an expression of rebellion against their no-smell, conformist heritage; more disposable money for nonessentials in dual-income households; . . . advertising and promotion associating fragrance with sports, good grooming, and national celebrity, especially designer names; and, lastly, American manufacturers becoming aware of marketing men's fragrances in ways that have made women's fragrances so successful."

Aramis had helped pioneer this particular wilderness. Having discovered a fertile and loamy soil, they were besieged by muscular squatters. Introducing a prestige fragrance in the late seventies meant expending between five and ten million dollars. *Nonetheless*, four major fragrances in this category were launched in 1978: Estée's own Devin; Ralph Lauren's Polo for Warner; John Weitz; and Karl Lagerfeld. The Weitz fragrance, expensive and exclusive, was backed by the same company that had done the popularly priced English Leather. An executive at English Leather explained, "We want to get a greater share of the department-store business, the fastest growing segment." Indeed, though all fragrances for men were selling, only the prestige market was *exceeding* the rate of inflation. Price didn't matter. And designer names were becoming like commodities. At Macy's

Herald Square flagship store, men's products made up five million dollars of the twenty-five-million-dollar annual sale of *all* cosmetics.

The Lauders must have been particularly shaken by the success of Ralph Lauren's Polo for Warner. George Friedman had been one of their own most talented executives, the brains behind Aramis. Before leaving Lauder, Friedman reportedly discussed the idea of developing a Ralph Lauren designer line under the Lauder aegis. He and Lauren went over to Warner only after the Lauders, the one-star family, turned thumbs down on the notion.

Estée and Leonard were furious with Friedman. He had been considered part of the family. But it was precisely because he was *not* part of the family that he went over to Warner, where he owned and controlled a good part of the action.

At Warner, Friedman recruited yet another creative and talented ex-Lauder executive, Robert Ruttenberg. Ruttenberg had been treasured by Estée in the six years he worked for her, even though she had never quite mastered the pronunciation of his name. "*Root*-enberg," she said to him once, "why were you talking to those *Revlon* people in the lobby?" Perhaps she had a point. Between Lauder and Warner, he had gone over to Revlon. He and Estée met again during that period: "*Root*-enberg," she asked, "how do you like working for Revlon?"

"It's wonderful," he said. "They're a group of imaginative and exciting people. I'm enjoying it."

"That's not possible!" Estée answered.

With the market expanding and the competition looming, the Lauders felt a need to make some kind of move to shore up and maintain the lead that their products for men had been enjoying all along. They perceived a problem in the image of the Aramis man as projected in their advertising. They were being forced to compete with the high profiles of the designers who had entered the fragrance market, men like Yves Saint Laurent, Ralph Lauren, and Oscar de la Renta. So the ax fell on AC&R, the small advertising agency that had grown up with Lauder. Lauder apparently felt that they had not done for their Aramis man what they had done for the Lauder woman. AC&R was permitted to retain the Estée Lauder and Clinique accounts, but Lauder began shopping around for a firm that could better represent their "potent, peppery" Aramis and their "country" Devin.

In the past a series of men had been used to represent Aramis. The first one looked lippy, arrogant, and bore an interesting resemblance to Ronald Lauder. He was pictured in a Lauderesque room. A woman in a miniskirt stood behind him chastely touching his shoulder. They both stared straight ahead, as in an old Flemish painting. He balanced two open books on his lap. The copy described his good life: "A retreat in the country . . . a portfolio of blue chips . . . Totally masculine. Designed for the man who knows his biggest advantage is a sense of style."

Then they flitted to other men. But they came back regularly to the exclusive use of boxes and bottles in their advertisements, boxes and bottles done in a German graphics style.

The other companies, mass and class, seemed to have a much easier time of it. English Leather had a five-dollar cologne featuring a sketch of a man and a woman right out of the *Kama Sutra*. Old Spice's couple appeared to be on the way to the bedroom. Revlon's popularly priced Chaz showed a fellow in dungarees walking robustly and joyfully with a bunch of daisies in his hands. Some of the bottle ads produced by the competition had bottles that were designed so priapically that they could have been launched not at Bloomingdale's but at Cape Canaveral. Such forthright messages would have been anathema to Estée's company. Once, when talking to a reporter, Estée had described Youth-Dew with a girlish mischievousness as "sexy" and then apologized for her vulgarity.

Ronald Lauder was thirty-four in 1978, the father of two little girls, Aerin and Jane. He lived right around the corner from Estée, on East Seventy-first Street. As vice-president of marketing and sales for all of Estée Lauder, Inc., it was up to him to find a replacement for AC&R. One of the first agency people he approached was Joe LaRosa of Waring & LaRosa, an agency that specialized in fashion and beauty. Many firms had wanted the Aramis account. LaRosa was thrilled to get it.

He liked Ronald's wry humor, and he liked the idea of working with creative, instinctual people who did virtually nothing in the way of dry marketing demographics. He and Ronald had a series of meetings. They discussed the kind of man who would most appropriately personify the sophisticated Aramis man; the kind of man who would most appropriately represent the countrified but nevertheless stinking rich and sophisticated Devin man. They talked about how best to take the Devin man off the printed page and put him on television. The Devin man had been pictured in better magazines for more than a year in verdant surroundings, a golden retriever at his side, a duck in his pond, a horse in his background.

They came up with the idea of creating an illusion around a tiny box. The television camera would first focus on the box and fool the viewer into thinking he was seeing a real scene: green fields, a duck, a distant horse. The camera would then pull back and reveal the illusion: The viewer had been seeing a box, after all, and not a real country setting.

LaRosa shot the commercial and previewed it for Ronald. They sat together in a screening room. As the spot ran, Ronald tapped LaRosa on the shoulder. "Mrs. Lauder would want me to tell you," he said, "that you *must never* do a Devin ad without a man in it."

LaRosa replied, "Tell Mrs. Lauder that if she can figure out how to get a man into that box, I'll shoot it."

With a dismaying consistency, LaRosa was forced to work on

copy that featured only boxes and bottles. "Very difficult," he remembers, "to write beautiful music under that."

Most frustrating of all to LaRosa was trying to figure out the pecking order at Estée Lauder, Inc. He never actually met Estée herself. He knew only that he and Ronald would agree to a concept and that it finally would be found unacceptable. "Obviously," he surmises, "someone was whispering in the prince's ear."

The LaRosa/Lauder alliance lasted less than a year. Toward the end of that time, LaRosa created a montage of Lauder products and standard characters: soaps, bottles, ducks, and a horse. He presented the work to Ronald. "These can be moved," he said. "Design your own ads."

LaRosa is still chairman and creative director of Waring & LaRosa, which now represents Aziza and Erno Laszlo cosmetics among others. He comments on the Lauders with an understanding ripened by the passage of time: "Sometimes, in advertising, a client comes to you and asks you to *hand* him his image; you function just like a shrink. The Lauders are just the opposite. The thing about them is that they know who they are. They're not verbal and can't express it very well. But they know who they are and especially who they are *not*. What they are is what Mrs. Lauder wants them to be, which is fine. You work their way or you don't work at all. Who would *presume* to tell them what to do?"

In 1979 Ronald took Marvin Davis and Frank Attardi to lunch at the "21" Club. The two men had their own agency, Attardi & Davis. Ronald said, among other things, that he was very influenced by German graphics. Frank Attardi, the designing half of the team, accordingly spent weeks working on a presentation with an emphasis on German graphics. He unveiled his presentation. Ronald walked around it, backed up, scrutinized. Then, without uttering one word, he left the room. Attardi was livid.

Marvin, who had grown up in New York City with Ira Levy's brother—Ira Levy was Lauder's creative vice-president—and was brought to the Lauders' attention because of that relationship, received a letter from Ira explaining how difficult Ronald was to work with and apologizing for the behavior. Attardi & Davis did eventually receive the assignment to represent the Aramis line. When Ira heard the news he hired a plane and a skywriter to write *Welcome Frank and Marvin*. When the day came for that expansive gesture, the sky was overcast. It didn't fly.

During Attardi & Davis's brief tenure, the search for the Aramis man continued. Ronald got more specific; he said the man should live in the East Sixties and jet around. He intended to recruit Horst, the brilliant fashion photographer, to work in the campaign. They didn't get Horst and they didn't find Mr. Right. Commercials with various models were shot. There was a loss of nerve. And a return to bottles and boxes. According to Davis, Leonard was in and out of the situation, swallowing Valium, prophesying his own doom: The business and Ronald were going to kill him: "If I don't get out of here, I'm going to die."

Davis, a man of passion who had worked beside Charles Revson at "the height of his cruelty," had a nightmarish time representing Aramis. He blistered over the Lauder indecisiveness. "We were never allowed to introduce a personality," he says, "because they were never sure who that personality should be. Estée had done it for the Estée line; she has not done it for her men's lines. After all our work, we ended up with bottle ads. That was safe. Nobody could say he was young or old or black or white. He was tortoise shell." Attardi & Davis lasted less than a year.

By 1981 a chastened AC&R was again representing the Aramis account. They, too, experimented with several Aramis men. In response to one of them, who was pictured sitting on the edge of a pool table, Marvin Davis sent a letter to Leonard. "I'm a heavy Aramis user," he recounts writing, "and I'm uncomfortable using

Aramis or displaying it in my bathroom knowing that this fey-looking schmuck is sitting on a pool table wearing my cologne." The model did not appear again.

AC&R soon convinced the Lauders to jettison the boxes and the bottles. There was a decision to settle on Ted Danson as the Aramis man. He appeared in all the commercials from 1981 until he left to do a television series in 1984. There was also an obviously joint decision that the Aramis ads were not so much lacking the right Aramis eyes as much as a degree of warmth. A campaign was initiated, for television and print, in which the Aramis man, after a decade of being alone, was *finally to look at the Aramis woman*: Kim Terry Masters. A relationship was begun.

Their first sexy commercial was shot at the Plaza Hotel. It was called "Meetings," the first generic television ad the company ever made; no store name ran under the picture. The piece was about a product and not a store sale. In the commercial he and she meet unexpectedly outside the hotel. He says she is more beautiful than ever and gives her a kiss on the cheek. She says that he had always known the right thing to say and observes that he is still wearing Aramis: "One of the nice things you did for me," he replies (implying, cleverly, that fragrance-wise, he is now on his own). It is established that these two gorgeous, successful people each has a plane to catch. He asks her what she's doing now. She replies: "I think I'm missing a plane."

When that thirty-second drama, one of several in a series, was shown in fifteen television markets during the 1980 Christmas season, Aramis sales went up 30 percent. Alvin Chereskin of AC&R called the creation of this campaign "a magic moment for all of us!"

The eighties were for the Lauders most people's thirties: sinuous sensuality, without removing a dinner jacket or loosening a tie. For the print campaign, it would be the Aramis man, tickled pink, standing with the Aramis woman in an awfully rich-looking hotel elevator. They are both in black. Her two chicly wrinkled Shar-Pei dogs (royal from China) sit at the end of long red nylon leashes, which are wrapped several times around his perfectly creased trousers.

From the inception of her company in 1947, Estée Lauder had been selling, as the cliché goes, not lipstick or fragrance but dreams. Fantasies. Ideals of beauty. But for every dream a dreamer is needed. Even Charles Revson had projected his own dampish dream in the slightly tartish and eminently available Fire and Ice women.

But whose energies, whose psychic reality had infused the Aramis man? Whose fantasy was he? Certainly not Estée's. The Lauder woman was her fantasy; in choosing Joe Lauder as her husband for life she demonstrated that the Aramis man was not even her type. Leonard's dream was success in business, a vital family company. And Ronald? He lived in the East Seventies. Joe Lauder was closer to pinochle than billiards.

Alone, the Aramis man was not only glacial but bloodless; not elegant but fey. He was no more vital than the boxes and bottles that he would haltingly and temporarily supplant.

The Aramis man needed a woman. And he needed to look at her and relate to her. When the company accepted that rather primitive notion, its advertising took on a look and a life that previously had been lacking.

Once again, with a stubborn, selectively attentive inner-directedness, the Lauders had stayed the course and maintained an almost ruthless integrity. Aramis had led and Aramis would lead in spite of young bloods and prodigal sons. Whoever was whispering in the prince's ear had smarts to spare.

Estée had, after all, figured out how to get the man into the box.

11

GIFT WITH PURPOSE

It was almost dusk—two weeks before Halloween 1979—when the doorbell of Estée's limestone mansion off Park Avenue was rung. A man wearing a chauffeur's uniform announced himself. "I'm here to pick up Mrs. Lauder," he said. "I'm the chauffeur."

According to the most cogent account of the incident, Estée's maid, Rose Nurse, opened the door and then queried Estée over the intercom. Estée was in her third-floor bedroom. Presently, Estée's real chauffeur-butler, forty-two-year-old John Drummond, confronted the stranger. "You're not the chauffeur," he said. *"I'm the chauffeur."*

The intruder brandished a gun. Two accomplices, one wearing a fake nose, the other a ski mask, shoved their way into the house. Rose Nurse somehow got to Estée, who locked her bedroom door. While one man tied Drummond to a radiator in the kitchen, taping his mouth shut, the other two bolted up the winding marble staircase and kicked down the locked door.

Estée, seventy-one years old, was hit across the face by one of the men. She opened two wall safes, whose contents included a great deal of valuable jewelry and paste copies of the originals. Estée and Rose were handcuffed to chairs, their heads covered with pillow cases. Keys to the handcuffs were placed on a desk. The men rummaged through a bureau drawer and found six thousand dollars in cash.

The bell rang again. The downstairs robber opened the door to interior designer Mark Hampton, who had decorated Estée's house in the south of France. He, too, was tied and taped.

At some point Estée finally had the presence of mind to wiggle over to the silent alarm, which had been placed on the floor for just such an occasion; she stepped on it. And so did they, fleeing without a trace.

The whole episode took fifteen minutes. By 5:30 P.M. local precinct police and/or the Holmes Detective Agency responded. A shocked and frightened Joseph Lauder returned from work shortly after.

For anyone, except the imperious Madame Rubinstein who had undergone a similar ordeal during her reign, such an experience is horrifying. For Estée, the horror was redoubled for its humiliating invasiveness. Police and investigative reporters are wont to ask questions more demanding than the sort posed as a rule by beauty editors, and here she could not mollify them with tips on makeup.

Estée's own version of the robbery appeared on the front page of the *New York Post* on October 17. The story headlined MILLION DOLLAR RIDDLE OF ESTÉE LAUDER, ran underneath the more prominent headline of that day: THE IRISH ARE PIGS, SAYS PRINCESS MEG. Estée's account to the newspaper was scoffing and blithe. She denied earlier reports—police reports among them—that the thieves had stolen a million dollars in jewels. She conceded the six thousand in cash. "I'm not a bit disturbed," she told the *Post*. "Luckily, I'd taken all my good things to the bank vault where I always keep them. They took a few things that were lying around, but nothing important."

The local precinct cops were as diplomatic and protective as possible in their responses to the press, and even omitted from their reports that she was tied up by the robbers. When a newsman pushed that issue, a police representative waffled, "Unconfirmed but possible." It was a higher-up from the chief of detectives who finally admitted that the jewelry may have been worth "as much as $1 million."

Estée did tell several friends subsequently that she had been tied up and hit. Agnes Ash of the Shiny Sheet in Palm Beach recounts, "She was very, very frightened because she was threatened with a gun and they did tie her to a chair. She was very afraid. She told me that."

For a time Estée would not allow herself to be photographed wearing any jewels at all. Since she was inclined to wear great hunks of stones all the time, that meant she was simply not photographed. And she made it a rule, after the robbery, to tell almost no one her traveling plans. Most significantly, she moved about accompanied by a bodyguard. Since the robbery she is guarded most of the time. Her house in New York has two protruding television cameras that wink red. When she is in Palm Beach, two guards in white uniforms—looking like Good Humor ice cream salesmen—stand prominently in front of her Georgian mansion.

The guards are out, people say. Estée must be in town.

The robbery was an unfortunate but virtually inevitable consequence of her enormously publicized if still very private life. In the late seventies and through the eighties she was in the social columns as often as any of the women she ever pursued. Her wealth was chronicled, her life-style flaunted. The robbery was a grievous experience but actually one of the few shadows cast in a charmed and buoyantly developing life. Her dreams—though open-ended—were one by one fulfilled. She danced into her remarkably healthy seventh decade like a kid at FAO Schwartz.

Honors of the sort she cared about were heaped upon her. In January 1978, her hazel eyes all misty, she received France's Legion of Honor (in spite of the fact that her fragrances were outselling Chanel's by three to one) for her generous contributions to the restoration of the Palace of Versailles. Communion-like, she wore a white Dior and carried a nosegay of red rosebuds as Gérard Gaussen, the consul general of France, pinned the medal on her, declaring, "Mrs. Lauder represents what we French admire most about Americans—brains and heart." Previous winners of Estée's caliber included Pierre Wertheimer, the legendary French perfumer who owned Chanel; Diana Vreeland; and Mary Lasker. More than 200 of her friends attended the ceremony at Gaussen's official residence on Fifth Avenue. Blanchette Rockefeller was there. And Ambassador and Mrs. Guilford Dudley. Grace Mirabella. Shirley Lord. And C. Z. Guest, who had forsaken the Hialeah opening.

A year later Estée, wearing a Givenchy, received the Gold Medal of the City of Paris, that city's highest honor. She was on a European tour launching Cinnabar in Paris, London, and Stockholm. Estée told Eugenia Sheppard, the society columnist who covered Estée as extensively as she had ever covered Jacqueline Kennedy, "It is not just business, but for me as a total person."

Hugh Carey, the governor of New York, gave her *and* Joe a Beautiful Apple Award. He suggested during the ceremony that since the state had a fruit of its own, a flower, and an animal, New York should begin considering adopting its own fragrance.

The Albert Einstein College of Medicine chose her as one of the nation's 100 Women of Accomplishment. Even the Fragrance Foundation honored her, in spite of the fact that she had, with customary insularity, refused to join the organization, which is simply an industry-wide association that promotes and educates on the subject of fragrance.

Richard Nixon offered her the ambassadorship to Luxembourg. She declined and blamed it on Joe. "I'm not going to carry her bags," he said.

Though she passed up that decidedly social sinecure (the post was the ambassadorship bestowed on Perle Mesta, "the hostess with the mostes' "), Estée's social aspirations never diminished. Her ambitions in the eighties, however, turned international.

118

The emphasis was on royalty. There was no more Duchess of Windsor in her life. The Duke had died and his widow was stricken by what is now known as Alzheimer's disease. (The Duchess has been living in Paris in seclusion since 1977. In June 1981 she passed her eighty-fifth birthday in bed, unable to receive visitors.) An ex-secretary to the Duchess, however, continues to harbor bad feelings toward Estée, believing that she deserted "Her Royal Highness" in a time of need and then crabbed to friends at tea parties how much the mad Duchess had cost her.

The former Grace Kelly, Princess Grace of Monaco, became one of the new focuses of Estée's attention. During the Christmas season in 1980 Estée and Joe received Grace and her daughter Princess Caroline in the New York mansion. Estée actually hired the Salvation Army band to play Christmas carols for the Princess and her thirty-odd guests. An enormous tree was decorated with old Viennese decorations. Douglas Fairbanks, Jr., sang Russian Christmas songs. (Estée's party for the Princess two years before had been attended by Nancy Reagan, accompanied by her "walker," Jerry Zipkin.)

All Estée's parties in the New York house begin on the third floor and gradually descend. By the evening's end, there is dancing on her grand and capacious marble floor on the first level. Frequently, there are dinner parties at which each guest has his own white-gloved footman standing behind his chair.

Estée also had eyes for Prince Charles of England, and she sponsored one of the polo matches in which he played. She watched with anxiety, worrying that the Prince might fall off his horse. When his engagement to Lady Diana Spencer was about to be announced, Estée tried to use her influence and her office in England to solicit an invitation to the wedding. Diana's father, the Earl of Spencer, was alleged to have balked at Joe Lauder's bold, uncharacteristic, and unsuccessful request: "If Prince Charles marries Lady Diana, will you invite us to the wedding?"

119

ESTÉE LAUDER

Estée covered most of her moves in every direction with private donations or, more frequently, foundation grants from the funding implement she and the family had established back in 1962. Called the Estée and Joseph Lauder Foundation, Inc., the gift-giving pattern it established over the years was, to some degree, the epitome of the foundation phenomenon, as once defined by Joseph C. Goulden in his book *The Money Givers*. "Foundations," he wrote, "are administered by philanthropoids who build cuckoo clocks and try to pass them off as cathedrals . . . building their childish sand castles on their private beaches."

In the seventies, Estée's foundation was targeting the tiny world of children's parks in New York City, most of which were ugly, asphalt, and gray, where youngsters were frequently injured falling from swings and seesaws. The Lauder Foundation earmarked several hundred thousand dollars for more imaginative, soft-form "adventure playgrounds," with sand everywhere to preclude injuries. Three Lauder parks were built all along the eastern rim of Central Park, the first two in affluent neighborhoods and the last, savvily, near Harlem.

The parks were widely publicized by her public relations department; they were always pointed out in the standard cook's tour of the Lauder offices, which tower over Central Park.

Estée's gift-giving has been criticized. Along with the Avon Products Foundation, the Revlon Foundation, and the Helena Rubinstein Foundation, the Estée and Joseph Lauder Foundation was taken to task by a feminist study group in the seventies for not targeting monies toward projects designed for women from whom, of course, their millions have been made. The Revson Foundation was designated the worst of the lot. A Revlon executive countered, "Charlie Revson did enough for women while he was alive—he made them beautiful."

On the subject of her charitableness generally, one very distinguished philanthropist observes, "Estée has been a very *canny* giver and she has gotten wonderful *mileage* from what she has put out. . . . Leonard has a conscience, but her giving has two prongs: publicity and to advance her career socially."

A Neiman-Marcus executive commented succinctly, "Estée was selfish *before* it became fashionable."

A more recent manifestation of Estée's self- and family-aggrandizing benefactions is the Lauder Foundation's role in the advancement of Ronald Lauder's ascendance in the New York museum world. In the year ending November 1982, the Foundation gave only $1,694 to the 100th Street Playground compared to $178,150 to the Museum of Modern Art and $95,000 to the Whitney Museum of American Art.

Ronald's special area is arms and armor. In 1981 the Lauder Foundation sponsored a medieval banquet at the Metropolitan Museum of Art for the triennial congress of the International Association of Museums of Arms and Military History. The organization brought together specialists in arms and armor from esteemed collections of the Tower of London and the Kremlin among others. For the curatorial types gathered, Ronald, an ardent collector himself of armor and German war memorabilia, conceived an authentic medieval feast, which included roast cockerel, mulled wine, beeves' broth, braided breads and bagels. Ronald, thrusting his arcane scholarship, maintained that bagels were staples in medieval Russia. The guests coveted the Met's distinguished collection. Ian D. D. Eaves, curator of The Armories of Her Majesty's Tower of London, smiled in the direction of several artifacts. A man named Hermes Knauer, a conservator at the Metropolitan, was the highlight of the evening, appearing in a full suit of late-fifteenth-century German armor. "A little bit of fantasy come true," he said.

Estée's fantasies are far less dicey, her simple pleasures simple. There is little evidence in her conversation of much reading. She does, however, enjoy books about the royal family of England. In

121

the early eighties she howled at the television antics of Archie and Edith Bunker in *All in the Family*. During her few quiet nights at home, Estée could watch the five o'clock, six o'clock, ten o'clock, and eleven o'clock news broadcasts, Joe pointing out to her that she was watching the same news four different times. She likes couture and clean, shiny floors. She enjoys taking her granddaughters out for a night on the town, or Leonard's boys to the polo matches. She loves her houses and holds on to all of them. Joe and Estée sometimes use their old house in Cannes as a place to change, a pit stop on their way to Abdulla and Zmira Zilke's grand seaside parties at Théoule.

She obviously enjoys expounding odd *bubameises* to the press, commingling the wit and wisdom of Mr. Belvedere and everybody's Aunt Fannie. In 1981 she told a reporter from the *Chicago Tribune*, "I never diet and I never take vitamins. It's a false way of eating. I believe in eating well. Everybody should have a pat of butter, for example. You need it for your bones, so they don't dry up. I have my pat for breakfast."

She has a habit of propounding in her own defense. Once, back in the seventies, she called a young executive into her office and told him that he wasn't traveling enough, that she wanted him on the road more. He demurred, being happily married and a father of two young children. "They need me," he said. She answered, "Nonsense, your children don't need you now. When they're fifteen, they'll need you."

Estée does very little exercising. Even in the south of France, where everybody builds pools, she did not. A friend comments, "I *hear* she went for a dip once at La Reserve [a very exclusive resort in the south of France]. She had on one of those Edith Lantz swimsuits, with the wires and the latex. She went for a dip and I think perhaps swam the length of the pool." At La Reserve, Estée had a conversation with Enid Nemy, the writer/socialite. Nemy said that she didn't like her own thighs. Estée said that she had the same problem. Nemy said she had conquered the problem by wearing colored tights under her bathing suit.

"That way I don't have to look at my thighs," Nemy said.

Estée said, *"What a good idea."*

Estée is noted for her discursive speech and her short attention span. She annoys all but the most inured or amused by her tendency to look past a specific person with whom she might be sitting. She cruises the room. One Palm Beach friend warned her once that if she didn't stop sizing up the cast of characters in the restaurant where they sat he was going to get up and leave. Another chuckles. "It's an annoying trait. But most people feel that she's entitled to be a character by now."

When asked whether Estée, the nose, had ever actually been in the fabled flower fields of Grasse, a social acquaintance responded, "Not in the way one might think, with a basket and streamers. I think probably she's been driven through Grasse in her limo. And where she lives at Cap Ferrat, the property is too expensive for fields of flowers."

Estée has never had the time or the leisure to cultivate the tastes and the talents of the class with whom she chose to consort. She hadn't spent a childhood perfecting the avocations of the monied and the leisured. If she had tried to pick up any French at all—she claimed to *Women's Wear Daily* that she spoke it fluently but Joe didn't—it was not obvious to her guests at Cap Ferrat, where her half of the table spoke English only, or English only was spoken to Estée. She was not even compelled to learn servant French because she regularly employed only Rose Nurse, an American woman, her maid, who served caviar on Ritz crackers.

Estée's happiest, certainly her most liberated times, were spent with Joe, her plain-spoken, tolerating, Rock of Gibraltar husband, who had a tendency, after a couple of drinks, to come perilously close to telling too much truth to the press. She would motion to him with a shushing finger on her lips. "Free speech.

Free speech," he joked. Primarily, however, it was he who kept her from going too far; he could close the door, sit her down, and talk sense to her. She respected Joe, always; their relationship seemed to get closer. A neighbor in New York remembers them on weekends when for some reason they had not gone to the country: "Walking hand-in-hand, just as cute as can be."

And Joe was a simple man. He liked war movies, fights, football, and baseball. He hated her parties, but he went to them on her behalf, imploring, as the evening wore on and him out, "Honey, can't we go home now?"

Estée is very mercantile and middle European in some of her ways. When she visits a shop where she has some of her dresses made, she sits in the back room with the help, her guard stationed outside. She shakes hands on entering and before leaving. She talked once to a Jewish seamstress there about the fact that she does all of her own cooking for the holidays; when the woman, however, responded too chummily, when she got too Jewish, Estée pulled back. Once that woman asked her simply: "Why aren't your products sold in Israel?"

Estée said, just as simply: "I can't and sell to the Arabs too."

Estée also mentioned Helena Rubinstein's facility in Israel—a somewhat anomalous defense when considering her normal attitude toward the competition.

Estée Lauder products are not sold in Israel, a subject that is seldom broached even by the internationally minded Leonard Lauder. When a research report on the Arab boycott was published in 1977, including a list of companies that were banned by the Arab League because they either traded with or built facilities in Israel, several Jewish-owned cosmetics companies were cited as prohibited from dealing in the Arab world on account of their relationship with Israel. Helena Rubinstein was on the Arab boycott list, and so was Revlon. Lauder was not. She had not traded with Israel.

Madame Rubinstein had built an enormous plant there in the early sixties at the request of the Israeli government. It is reported now to be Rubinstein's most profitable overseas factory. Revlon also has a plant there. Doyle, a Revlon executive, claims they could make more money trading with the Arabs, that when he was with Borghese, a Revlon line, the Middle Eastern Iranians wanted to import the product and he was compelled to tell them that was impossible because they were on the list. Doyle maintains that Mickey Soroko, one of Revson's chums and the son of an orthodox rabbi, years ago "convinced Charles that he, as a Jew, *had* to have a plant in Israel. Revlon products are on the ban list; Estée's are not."

Allan Mottus points out that *internationally* Lauder was a late starter compared to Rubinstein and Revlon. "From a business point of view," he says, "I don't think they [Lauder] had many options. . . . Her fragrances apparently do very well in the Middle East. They do like those heavier, pungent fragrances."

Aramis, according to a competitive executive, is "mostly profitable internationally. Huge amounts are sold to the Arabs. They won't sell to Israel or they'll be blacklisted."

Leonard must be badly conflicted on the issue. He is known to have recruited his friends to support the candidacy of former Senator Jacob Javits because of Javits's strong stance on Israel. In addition, the Lauder Foundation, of which Leonard is an important officer, has continuously contributed large sums of money to Jewish and Zionist charities: $90,000 to United Jewish Appeal in 1976/1977; $25,000 to the Jewish National Fund in 1981; $154,000 to the United Jewish Appeal in 1982.

Beyond the fact that she knew that selling to the Arabs precluded her selling to the Israelis, Estée's political feelings are unclear. Beyond the enormous pride that she derives from her friendship with First Lady Nancy Reagan, it is doubtful that Estée is much of a political animal.

Her priorities have always been family, social elevation, and business—the fragrance part of which she has never abandoned. In the summer of 1981, for instance, she was leading her lush life but thinking also of a name for the new men's fragrance line her company was about to launch. She was stumped. "The name for the new one has to signify clean, elegant, divine, sophisticated," she said. "All of these things. But it will come. I'll think of it."

12

J.H.L.

She called the new fragrance, which had woodsy and floral notes, J.H.L. For Joe, of course: Joseph Harold Lauder. Many claims issued forth from the Lauder organization about J.H.L. Estée said she had wanted something fresh: "I didn't want a fragrance that preceded your entrance. I wanted something that would warm with you." Ira Levy, whom some had taken to calling Estée's "dauphin" because he was like another son to her—one who traveled the world in search of aesthetic inspiration for packaging the products—claimed to have based the whole J.H.L. *look* on Joe's habiliments: the flacon after his sherry decanter, some of the store display units after his eighteenth-century Sheraton dressing table, the outer carton by the silk lining of one of his dressing jackets.

The fragrance was launched with great success at Saks Fifth Avenue and at London's Harrods in October 1982. The suggested price was $30 for 1.7 ounces of cologne. J.H.L. was an Aramis product, but top of the line. Classic Aramis cologne sold at $12.50 for 2 ounces.

This was an obvious reaction to the profusion of designer fragrances on the counters, using every possible advantage that accrued to the Lauder name. Other Aramis products had been marketed with no reference to Estée Lauder, the woman or the company; this time, the connection was stressed. Advertising recounted how this "well-mannered, custom-blended cologne" was created by Estée for the most important man in her life. Ira Levy raved to the press, "How romantic and honest to have a fragrance created by one woman for one man!" And Ronald cracked, "This was done by Mrs. Lauder, whom we consider a great perfumer, as opposed to being done by a famous tailor." (He was obviously not mindful of a famous tailor named Coco Chanel, who'd had a fairly good run with a designer fragrance.)

Joe was honored and hopeful. "It's a very elegant idea. And I'm flattered," he said.

What the role of the eponymous Joe was intended to be in the promotion of the fragrance is not clear. With some making over, especially of his perenially tired, furrowed gaze—he could have assumed a visible presence. Joe had gentle, vintage good looks, of the Sidney Blackmer variety. His wily wife seemed to have had something in mind. For instance, she was easing him—or at least the idea of him—ever so gently into the corporate press tour.

It should be understood that there were no wasted moves when the press came calling. Estée choreographed every step along the way: There were the deftly interruptive telephone calls from, say, a maharanee; there were drop ins from executives with messages about their latest products; even the makeovers she did on the women reporters had the effect of deflecting their attention away from frivolous questions like: Where were you born? But Estée, before the introduction of J.H.L., never referred to Joe's office in their headquarters at the General Motors Building. He surely must have had one, but he was never there, always at the plant in Melville, Long Island. When the fashion editor of *The Times-Picayune* in New Orleans visited in July 1982, Estée led her through Joe's "all wood-paneled and masculine office." Of course, he wasn't in it. However, the stage was obviously being set for his assuming the kind of public identity that he had never before enjoyed.

It's hard to assess how Joe Lauder would have shouldered a greater visibility. By 1982 Estée had been a kind of celebrity for several years, and he seemed not to experience that as a problem. The exception that proved the rule occurred one night in Palm Beach when he and Estée were dining with two friends at the restaurant of the Colony Hotel. Estée had originally set up the couples' reservations at another hotel, using the woman's name while setting up the arrangements. The woman was better known than her husband, whom she had recently married, and she was the one Estée knew better. When the husband learned that his reservation had been made under his wife's name, he became so resentful that he insisted they change over from the first hotel to the Colony, which annoyed Estée because she'd had a basket of fruit sent to the first hotel. The four of them were now sitting at the Colony discussing spousal celebrity. Joe was lecturing the younger man about the situation, advising him to take pride in his wife's achievements, to dispense with the old masculine hang-ups. And as Joe went on about modern marriage, the sommelier brought their wine to the table, walking directly to Estée. He offered the bottle for *her* approval; he poured the first tasting into *her* glass.

Joe rose, excused himself, and repaired to the bar area, followed by the other aggrieved husband. They had a couple of belts at the bar before returning to the corking problem at hand.

Joe apparently did enjoy his booze. It made a good deal of his social life endurable: the endless functions and parties he was obliged to attend in his role as Lauder executive and as Estée's escort. There was an event one evening at Bloomingdale's, for instance, the first step of which necessitated listening to an address by store executive Marvin Traub. It wasn't party time yet, so the liquor bar was covered. Harry Doyle was among the guests and thinking about how much he wanted a drink. Whereupon he caught sight of Joe, standing with a glass of scotch in his hand.

"How the hell do you get a drink around here?" he asked Joe.

"You bring your own," Joe answered. "Would you like a sip?"

As a businessman, of course, Joe realized the necessity of the business function. He chafed a bit when the event was more about Estée's pleasure than the Lauder business. He told a society columnist once, as he glanced around at the glitz and the glitter, "You know, I've never been impressed by any of this." She responded, "I never thought you were, Joe." At the end of the countless evenings out, he'd call for the car and remind Estée of the lateness of the hour. Someone who attended many parties with them remembers Joe's attitude: "He could have strangled her, of course, for bringing him out again when he really wanted to be home with his feet up. But when he looked at her his little face would light up and he'd say, 'Doesn't Estée look *great* tonight.' "

Joe had a quiet, sardonic humor, which sometimes rattled Estée. They were at a dinner party and a small-talking guest said to him that she had just bought a Lauder lipstick. "I'm glad you did," he said. "We need the business." Estée felt compelled quickly to reassure the woman that business was really very healthy.

He was a hard-working, equable man. People liked him. A friend who socialized with Joe and Estée for more than a decade remembers only one occasion when he displayed any temper or meanness of spirit. And that happened because a waiter bumped into one of his sons. Joe was fiercely loyal and protective on behalf of his family.

Joe talked to *Women's Wear Daily* in early January 1983 on the subject of raising children. He recalled that when Leonard and Ronald were away at school or in military service, he regularly sent them copies of all Lauder company correspondence. When they complained about the amount of reading he was thrusting on them, he told them to do as much as possible. "You get out what you put in" was Joe's advice on life in general.

The maxim was applicable with a vengeance to the fortunes of Estée Lauder, Inc., which, in 1982, was approaching an estimated billion-dollar mark globally, making Estée's company the largest privately held cosmetics company in the world. Lauder was even beginning to threaten Revlon's numbers; Revlon beauty-product profits sagged in 1981 for the first time in the company's history. Mike Blumenfeld, vice-president of Bloomingdale's New York, expressed the generally held conversation that "Lauder is always the [competition's] enemy. It is the leader."

Lauder moved into the seven-digit category just as Leonard, forty-nine, was made chief executive officer of the company, and Ronald, thirty-eight, chairman of Lauder International. The mantles were shifted around at a press gathering that Estée called to announce the promotion of her "sweet boys"—an occasion she used also to assess her competition. She told *The New York Times*: "Lancôme is nothing." She complained that her competitors periodically raided her staff in search of talent, but that after "three, six months, they run out of my ideas."

On the subject of the personal demise of all the historic competitors: Charles Revson, Helena Rubinstein, and Elizabeth Arden, Estée said, "I'm the only one left. Thank God."

The Lauder priority under Leonard was becoming research and development in skin care. Much of the R&D was being done in collaboration with a West German laboratory that was doing general research in skin-cell repair and with another outside laboratory that was experimenting in the uses of hyaluronic acid as a moisture preserver. The two areas would result in the creation of one of the company's most successful skin-care formulations, Night Repair.

And increasingly, under Leonard, the company was expanding its international markets. In England Estée Lauder enjoys a success and a reputation equal to what she has achieved in the United States. When the high-tech skin care Lauder subsidiary, Prescriptives, made its debut there at Harrods in 1980, a beauty writer for *The Times* of London commented: "The system doesn't come cheap, but then nor does psychiatry, which is what the customer will feel she's had by the time a Lauder-trained skin analyst has examined her skin under special lighting, asking the sort of questions that makes most minds turn instantly blank, probed gently but persistently for special problems, including stress (type unspecified, you supply your own) and finally issued an individual prescription for cleansing, 'energising' and protecting . . . Too soon to pronounce judgment, but Mrs. Lauder does have the irritating habit of producing expensive treatment items that *are* that bit better than the perfectly good ones that we sensible consumers ought to be using."

Lauder's fastest growth was happening in Spain; their most nettlesome problems encountered on account of the Japanese trade barriers. In 1981 their estimated international volume in seventy-five countries was over four hundred million dollars. Leonard was planning to make Estée Lauder a household word throughout the world.

Like his mother, Leonard meshed his business and his social activities. He and Evelyn, a vice-president of Estée Lauder, Inc., built a chalet in Aspen, Colorado. Leonard became a major contributor to and participant in the Aspen Institute for Humanistic Studies, a sort of think tank, seminar and recreation area for business executives. They issue position papers about world affairs and conduct executive seminars for which executives prepare by reading Plato and Milton Friedman. "The most exclusive boys club in the world" is how one former staff person describes the group.

In November 1982, Leonard traveled to China for the institute. Revlon, Max Factor, and Avon already had facilities there. Leonard returned and commented, "They're not ready for us, but they will be." He stated that when China was ready, Clinique would be dispatched first. But he did perceive a real need for his skin-care products there: "Chinese boys and girls have very bad skin."

Ronald's promotion in 1982 appeared to be planned to fulfill his larger destiny outside the company. From 1980 to 1983

Ronald had been extremely active on the New York State Republican Finance Committee; he was credited with helping to raise four million dollars in the state to pay GOP campaign debts. By November 1982 he was being considered for a job in the Defense Department. President Ronald Reagan's personnel director told *The Washington Post*, "We want him on board. But we don't know exactly where. He's philosophically in line with the president, and is a capable, proven manager." The director assured the *Post* that Estée's friendship with Nancy Reagan had nothing to do with Ronald's prospect.

Estée's and Joe's sweet boys comfortably ensconced, their business preeminently sweet, the couple prepared to celebrate the fifty-third anniversary of their marriage of January 15, 1930. A weekend was planned: They would dine with the boys and their families at Leonard's apartment on East Sixty-seventh Street on Friday night and then at Ronald's on East Seventy-first Street on Saturday.

On Wednesday of that week Joe was running a fever, so a social engagement was cancelled. By Friday, however, he was well enough for Leonard's dinner. That Saturday, which was the actual anniversary, they went to Ronald's elegant duplex for a quiet family dinner with the boys, their wives, and the four grandchildren. During the evening Joe complained of not feeling well. As he was leaving, just before midnight, Joe, eighty, collapsed. He was pronounced dead on arrival at Lenox Hill Hospital.

There was a small, private service for him at the Riverside Chapel that Sunday, January 16. Then he was buried in Estée's family plot at Beth-El Cemetary, which her family had once owned and where her father Max had worked. Joe's epitaph: *The most wonderful man in the world. Loved by all. Kind husband. A great father and devoted grandfather. Dec. 25, 1902–Jan. 15, 1983.*

Fog rolled over his obituaries. Even *The New York Times*, which ran a big picture and two half-columns, issued mist and misinformation. His age was stated as "in his 70s"; no marriage date, no birth date, no information about services or place of interment. There was one reference to Estée's Viennese uncle.

More revelatory was the flotsam that surfaced after the obit ran. In that part of the newspaper devoted to the paid expressions of regret by people and institutions, there were condolences paid by the Mohegan Park Jewish Center, of which Leonard was a founding member. The Queens League of Camp Sussex expressed its regrets at Joe's passing, as did the president of Temple Emanu-El, where Joe and Estée had worshiped with their family on the High Holy Days. And the Angel of Mercy Committee of Palm Beach expressed deep sympathy to Estée.

Joe's will, which had been made in 1963 and then slightly revised in 1978, simply redistributed his shares in the business so that Ronald's voting and nonvoting shareholdings were made equal in number and kind to Leonard's. The Lauder empire was kept virginal and intact and *per stirpes*. Nothing was left to the daughters-in-law. Legacies of $25,000 apiece went to one nephew, Paul Lauter, an academic and civil libertarian, and two nieces.

Estée was devastated by Joe's sudden death. After the burial, she stayed with Ronald for several weeks, sleeping in one of her granddaughter's bedrooms on the top floor of the duplex. She withdrew from the business, apparently unable to conceive of a time when she would be whole enough for work of any sort. She could not bear to think of returning to the south of France without him. Ida Stewart, a Lauder vice-president who had been with Estée for twenty-three years, functioned during this mourning period as a kind of companion and lady-in-waiting.

Harry Doyle and his wife encountered Estée and Ida at a performance of *My One and Only*, the Broadway musical. The Doyles were seated three rows behind them; they had sent an "ecumenical mass card" to Estée when they received word of Joe's death, and that had touched her deeply. When Harry approached her during the intermission he put his arms around her to express his sorrow. Estée wept softly, "Oh my God, Harry, how can I go on without him?"

She stayed with Ronald a great deal during this period. She was at his vacation home in Bridgehampton, Long Island, out walking on a country path alone, when, according to a friend of Robert Ruttenberg of Warner Cosmetics, Ruttenberg zoomed past her on his motorcycle. Seeing his ex-boss, he slowed to a halt and dismounted, in full gear and goggles. Realizing that he had terrified her, he pulled off his goggles.

"Oh, it's you *Root*-enberg," Estée said with relief. "You startled me."

The friend was told that they stood on that peaceful country lane: Road Runner and the bereaved Cosmetics Queen, talking intimately. She told him how very lonely she was; he told her about his recent divorce. They were together for more than an hour.

A month later she met him at a black-tie affair. She seemed unresponsive. "Hello, Mrs. Lauder," he reportedly said. "Don't you know who I am?"

She said, "Yes, I know who you are. I saw you on the motor-cycle."

And she walked over to some more important social type.

Estée was herself again.

13

BEYOND THE MAGIC

Joe is missed still. And that loss no doubt exacerbates Estée's feelings about Ronald's removal to what appears to be a permanent place on the Washington scene. Soon after his father's death in 1983, Ronald accepted a post under Secretary of Defense Caspar Weinberger as deputy assistant secretary, European and NATO Policy. He now works at the Pentagon. He described his duties to Jane Perlez of *The New York Times* as including "negotiating with the British on how American troops there should be housed." He added, "I don't see cosmetics and defense as being a major conflict of interest." An anonymous "diplomat from a NATO country" told Perlez for the piece, "He doesn't really know anything but he says so up front." (Ad man Joe LaRosa, who worked under Ronald briefly trying to put the Devin man in a box, reacted to Ronald's new defense position, "Good God! Does that mean he's counting missiles?")

Estée's younger son is taking speech lessons and entertaining political notions beyond the Pentagon. According to a family friend, "Ronald *does* have very serious political ambitions. He sees himself as a kind of renaissance man: Nelson Rockefeller—power, politics, and art. And I'm sure he has the best brains money can buy behind him. Estée, however, is *not* 100 percent for it. She'd like it if she could say, 'My son the President'; on the other hand, she'd really like him back in her business, nearby."

During his service under the first Reagan administration, Ronald's wife Jo Carole, commuted to and from Washington while maintaining their residence in New York City; he was headquartered temporarily at the Watergate. They have since moved to Washington and have bought a house in Georgetown, which they furnished in English country style.

Ronald has befriended certain political powerbrokers like Roy Cohn and his law partner, Tom Bolan. And it was through the former, who gave a dinner for forty at a Washington restaurant, that Estée encountered outgoing United Nations Ambassador Jeane Kirkpatrick. Mrs. Kirkpatrick was wearing a black-and-gold metallic knit jacket. According to *WWD*, Estée approached the usually crisp and unflappable ambassador. "You should wear blue or red," she told her. Estée pointed out her own blue Oscar de la Renta jacket. "It's very young," she said. A somewhat stunned Jeane Kirkpatrick replied, "You mean you don't like what I'm wearing?"

Estée is to all intents and purposes retired from the business, though Leonard, out of deference, still consults with her on fragrance. But the corporation is, in every regard, spearheaded by Leonard, with Estée now more queen mother than queen.

The business of cosmetics, about which she taught the ABC's on merchandising, sell-thru, gift-with-purchase, and entrepreneurial chutzpah, has grown almost beyond her ken. She began in skin care when she marketed John Schotz's formulations; Clinique was the first breakthrough, appealing to the expanding and expandable demand for products that improved rather than adorned the skin. But the market whose primer she helped write has taken a quantum leap into high-tech and so-called science, which may make her retirement timely and fortuitous.

This new surge in skin care began in the early eighties when the baby-boom population, who were then approaching forty, began to age. Business is reacting to the oxymoron proposition that nothing is more elastic than aging skin.

The market in general is awash with promises of protracted youthfulness. They may not work as proclaimed; they may be tap dancing on the roof. But they are beyond anything Estée could have imagined when she was peddling Uncle John Schotz's early all-purpose creme.

The September 1984 issue of *Drug & Cosmetic Reporter* rolled off these treatment products trippingly as examples of the copywriters' art and the industry's disposition: Clarifiance Hydrating Fluide and Solution Specifique Spot Control (Lancôme), Hydro-Minerali Revitalizing Eye Creme (Princess Marcella Borghese), Visible Difference Eye-Fix with Primilin III (Elizabeth Arden), Issima Concentrated Revitalizer With Hydrolasting (Guerlain), Demaquillant Aqua-Purifiant (Chanel), Skin Renewal Therapy Lotion (Alexandra de Markoff), Overnight Success (Coty), Cellular Cycle Ampoules (La Prairie), Multi-Regenerante Rich Treatment Cream (Clarins), Smoothing Body Scrub (Elysée), Suractif Plus Multiactif Revitalizer (Lancaster), Night Support Skin Revitalizing Formula (Avon), and Intensive Wrinkle Treatment Complex (Kelemata).

All epigones compared to Lauder's sensationally successful Night Repair, introduced in 1983 and proclaimed, by a Lauder executive, as the strongest treatment item in the company's history. An executive at Dayton's in Minneapolis called it a "phenomenal item"; in department store after department store it emerged as the biggest-selling product of its kind.

Leonard's business is doing just fine. One wonders, however, what Estée *really* thinks of creams that act in the night. Once, commenting on her first product, John Schotz's Super-Rich All-Purpose Creme, marketed by Estée in the forties, she exclaimed, "It's all-purpose because I don't believe in night cream. How does a cream know it's dark outside?"

This newer, more knowledgeable product, Night Repair, was advertised as a revolution in skin care. In the very effective black-

and-white print ads, there appears a full-page picture of a sleeping beauty, her night table elegantly appointed with a gold pen, flowers, and a tiny television set. The copy reads:

"Night Repair is a *biological breakthrough* that uses the night, the time your body is resting, to help speed up the natural repair of cells that have been damaged during the day by the ultraviolet light all around us (which incidentally occurs all year long, winter as well as summer). Night Repair also greatly increases the skin's ability to hold moisture."

Through its various lines, Estée Lauder, Clinique, Aramis, and now Prescriptives, in department store after department store, Estée's skin-care products have been primarily leaders, outselling competitive products positioned similarly. By virtue of its track record and its aggressive advertising claims, Lauder is the bellwether, ringing out messages, more scientific-sounding than ever before, that the appearance of youth is protractable, indeed recoverable, through the nourishing, hydrating renewal of the cells of the skin.

Many dermatologists do not consider these claims valid or their science well grounded. They deny that skin can be nourished, fed, or the like, or that the so-called active ingredients the industry is discovering one after the other can penetrate the outer layer and scratch where aging skin really itches.

Even Dr. Norman Orentreich himself, the medical pioneer of Clinique, has drawn the line unequivocally: "There is no topical preparation affecting the outermost layer of the stratum corneum that the FDA will allow you to call a cosmetic that will work," he told *Drug & Cosmetic* in September 1984.

Dr. Albert M. Kligman, professor of dermatology at the University of Pennsylvania School of Medicine, who sits in a chair endowed by Leonard Lauder, comments on the Lauder skin-care products, "Lauder makes good products, no doubt about it," says Dr. Kligman, whose special interest is aging skin. "Their products are no less safe than anyone else's; and most products made by the big cosmetics companies are quite safe. It's the claims that put them into the stratosphere. The claims would be very hard to substantiate. If the FDA had more money and time, then what Estée Lauder does would bring them under scrutiny. Puffery is understood, but there are boundaries. And it looks as if Lauder may exceed these boundaries. It's almost as if these things were being used to treat disease. Or the strong inference is that these are prophylactics that will prevent you from getting wrinkled or aged. They use words that suggest that you are really using drugs: Prescriptives. And I know that their competitors are dragged into making similar products they don't feel too good about."

The irony is that now is precisely the time when straight talk about topically applied skin care could be most effective. Ronald Reagan's recent bout with skin cancer made clarion clear once again the direct relationship of basal cell carcinomas and exposure to sun. Word has come down repeatedly from the medical profession that the most significant cause of aging skin is exposure to the ultraviolet rays of the sun. Dr. Barbara Gilchrest, professor of dermatology at the Harvard Medical School, asserts; "All the change that we think of as aging—the wrinkling, the blotching, the bumps—isn't aging at all. It is sun damage."

In response to these kinds of pronouncements, an increasing number of manufacturers of skin-care preparations *and* cosmetics are adding shields against harmful rays of the sun to their products. Estée's Tinted Day Creme and Lancôme's Bienfait du Matin, both heavily advertised, are foundationlike products that contain screening elements.

But the messages are mixed with more than a touch of avarice. At the same time that Lauder—among others—is implying that sunlight can be hazardous to health and good looks, it is encouraging women to go out and bake in the sun until they look as gorgeous as the evenly tanned Lauder woman who was featured prominently in every important fashion/status magazine in the spring and summer of 1985 wearing a white maillot by Connie Banks. The product the company was pushing through that particular advertisement is called Estée Lauder Sun, a Golden Sun Pre-Tan Accelerator. It contains Biotan™, actually a whole group of amino acids, one of which is tyrosine. The consumer is instructed to use the product for several days before going out into the sun; the tyrosine is acting during that time to speed up the production of melanin, the pigment that leads to tanning.

During July 1985, Betty Furness, who does a consumer segment on NBC's *Today* show, became interested in the product. She asked the Lauder people to appear in a feature about Estée Lauder Sun. Not surprisingly, they declined. She invited two dermatologists, Dr. Nelson Novack and Dr. Dawn Greewald, who read the material provided by the company about the product. Dr. Novack maintained, on camera, "Tyrosine is the precursor . . . of melanin, the pigment that can lead to a tan. Their contention is that this product will accelerate the tan. To the best of my knowledge, no medical literature exists yet to substantiate this." Dr. Greewald contended, "You have to prove that more tyrosine equals more melanin, and I don't think that the proof is in yet."

But, of course, the dazzling Lauder model, sprawled across three-quarters of a double-page spread, wasn't talking tyrosine. She was saying burn is beautiful. When Betty Furness asked the doctors whether there was a reason *not* to use the product, they both stated that no product is any good if it encourages people to go out into the sun.

Since the FDA under the administration of Ronald Reagan has been notoriously sluggish and done virtually nothing to curtail the new breed of "scientific," high-tech skin-care merchandise, it will finally be up to Leonard Lauder to use the enlightenment he has presumably refined with his Aspen Institute reading lists to choose between the public interest and that of Estée Lauder, Inc.

———

In other of its choices, Lauder has behaved with irresolution. The Lauder look remains lily white despite the fact that their market, for fragrance especially, is emphatically black and white. *Essence*, a magazine for upscale black women, wooed and finally (but temporarily) won a major victory when *Clinique* placed several advertisements in 1985. The most obvious conflicts were precluded by the fact that Clinique advertisements never feature people, only products. The editors were delighted, not only for the revenues provided but for the barriers that might have been broken through the appearance of the Clinique presence. (Revlon does advertise, using black models, which is *Essence*'s policy. But that came only after a long-haul hassle in the Revlon corridors.) Additionally, *Essence* approves of Clinique. A spokeswoman commented, "Their hypo-allergenic line is excellent for the various skin types that black women have. . . . And we were, for a time, the biggest stray from the image of the Lauders."

It was a stray that the company must have felt as too radical. By August 1985 the Clinique advertisements were discontinued. Amelia Bassin, who was at that time preparing an article called "Un-ethical Us," lambasted the decision as it reflected the white/black schism in cosmetics advertising: "There are almost no fragrance ads in *Essence*, and I think that's disgusting. And *Essence* has a very good market. I think it's racist for the big advertisers to stay out of black publications."

All of the decisions that Leonard will be compelled to make now without his mother will be made in a marketplace where the competition is fiercer than at any time since the Estée Lauder–Charles Revson wars. After a decade of unchallenged preeminence, Lauder is faced with the specter of another company—or a confederation of companies—whose stated purpose is the aggressive expropriation of Lauder's domination of the class department store market. The industry watches with keen interest.

The competition's roots literally go back to hair dye, whose profits, almost eighty years ago, built the publicly owned French company, L'Oréal. L'Oréal's brand names came to include Lancôme, Guy Laroche, and Cacharel. Between 1979 and 1984, L'Oréal grew at an amazing rate, posting, according to *Forbes* magazine, "annual compound revenue growth of 20.8%, more than triple the 6% growth rate of number one Avon ($3 billion sales) and better than double the 9% rate of number two Revlon (about $2.4 billion sales)." L'Oréal's licensed distributor in the United States is Cosmair, a private company in New Jersey that made a small fortune by cornering the hair mousse market. L'Oréal, to sweeten the pot, is held in part by Nestlé's. Allan Mottus has called Nestlé's, "L'Oréal's 'Swiss godfather.' "

There was nothing for Lauder to worry about in the expansion of this confederation, whose interests appeared to be solely in the mass toiletries market. But in 1983 there was talk that Warner Cosmetics, at that time headed by George Friedman and Robert Ruttenberg, was up for grabs. Warner Cosmetics included quality fragrances by Ralph Lauren (Polo and Chaps) and Gloria Vanderbilt. Rupert Murdoch showed interest and then lost it. Cosmair was bidding, at which point a concerned Leonard Lauder demonstrated some interest in buying the company himself. Warner Cosmetics, however, on Friday the thirteenth in January of 1984, went to Cosmair for $146 million.

Lancôme may indeed have been "nothing" when Estée dismissed the company to *The New York Times* in 1982, but now it is part of a confederation of companies and licenses that have virtually limitless money, the time-tested allure of French products, and an animating motivation, bold and energetic. Jean Levy, Cosmair's president, has targeted the department stores, and he is after the ruling establishment there, which is generally understood to be Lauder. "They're going to have to fight every day for this," he told the *Times* in mid-1985. "Their leadership isn't perennial—it isn't given by heaven or God."

In addition to everything else, the French-connected confederation has George Friedman and Robert Ruttenberg, both of
whom learned while playing on the Lauder team by both nega-
tive and positive example; and they are unencumbered by Lauder
strictures. Ruttenberg wants Aramis. He told *Women's Wear Daily*
in April 1982, before the Cosmair deal, "In some branch stores
there are two cases for men's fragrances. One is for Aramis and
the other is for the thirty other brands." This he means to change,
using Polo's success as leverage. The situation was in the process
of being changed by August 1984, when Allan Mottus reported
that "while all Aramis products, including Aramis 900, Devin,
and J.H.L., controlled 26.4 percent of the market, showing a
9.5 percent gain, Polo/Chaps scored a 15 share of the market,
showing a 26.9 percent growth."

Cosmair is working on several levels. A Warner executive who
was visiting a department store in the midwest in 1985 was
talking, Estée Lauder–style, about pulling his line if his real
estate was not expanded in the store. He commented arrogantly,
"Managers of stores are smart professional people now. Not those
old ladies who go to dinner all the time. Too much of their
business is in Estée Lauder, and they recognize that as unhealthy.
They want to build up new businesses. We represent that oppor-
tunity.

"We are now a threat in every area. Lancôme is threatening
Lauder in cosmetics. Polo is threatening Aramis. Lauren is
threatening Lauder fragrances. And there's all that European
money. We want to be number one. We are absolutely determined to do it better than they did. She's very rigid in her
thinking. It's all emotion." And then the almost unthinkable
remark, "Her ways are yesterday's news."

Don Davis, editor of *Cosmetics Insiders' Reports*, observes,
"Friedman and Ruttenberg really know the business. If I were
Lauder I'd be considerably worried about what Warner could
eventually do to me."

The next few years will determine whether the smart professional people can supplant the old ladies who go to dinner and whether the beauty consumer really requires the charismatic presence of a personality such as Estée and her entrepreneurial predecessors, whether the magic—even in high-tech skin care—can work independently of the magician.

It is certain that there will be experimentation on every level. Untrammeled by Estée Lauder's early sense of class, Warner and the others might even set about to change the concept of class, coining new money in a sort of utilitarian, lumpen elitism. Cosmair is selling pricey lines at drugstores. L'Oréal cosmetics are selling at 20 to 30 percent higher than the mass products in the same drug stores: Class products in a mass environment for the busy woman and man who want French allure where they buy their mouthwash.

Allan Mottus has called the group at Cosmair "heavy-handed and confrontational." But Mottus has a soft spot for entrepreneurs with ragged edges. He even liked Charles Revson; Revson called the young man, then a reporter for *Women's Wear Daily*, "Words" because he was so good with them. And Mottus has a certain fondness for Estée and Leonard. When Mottus broke his leg badly in 1974, Leonard called him regularly when he was laid up at St. Vincent's Hospital in New York City and arranged for him to be treated by Dr. Howard Rusk of the Rusk Institute. Leonard sent him books, including *Watership Down*. Estée telephoned him to ask, "Darling, how are you feeling?"

"I can't get around too well," he told her.

"Don't worry about it," Estée assured the young man. "You've got a good head on your shoulders."

Even now Estée is a quick thinker. Her head remains a puzzlement to just about everyone. She gets around with amazing vigor, a juggernaut at seventy-seven. Friends remark that she has never looked better or svelter than she does now. She apparently has abandoned her self-serving notion that most American women are too thin. She cries still about Joe's death, and she visits his grave with some regularity.

She appears at company functions when her matrilineal presence is required; and, of course, with the threat of L'Oréal, that presence is crucial, but daughter-in-law Evelyn is always present and increasingly accounted for. She is obviously gradually assuming Estée's figurehead and functionary role. Just how important that kind of symbol will be in the increasingly high-tech tone of the modern cosmetics world remains to be seen.

Estée's last big professional show accompanied the launching of Lauder for Men: "A fragrance so distinctive it transcends time and space." She *and* Evelyn—the fact was made eminently clear in all the nicely managed press accounts—invited 100 of the handsomest men in New York to lunch at the Helmsley Palace. They included John Fairchild, Ambassador Francis Kellogg, Jerry Zipkin, Thomas Hoving, Marvin Traub, Andy Warhol, and Allan Mottus. The luncheon was done with typically impeccable Lauder style. Each table represented a fashionable world capital. Menus were printed on expensive napkins that could be taken home as souvenirs. Everyone had a gift. And the coverage was predictably expansive. Estée, who looked superb under the closest scrutiny, demonstrated the old Lauder technique for selling fragrance. She spritzed, "If you don't smell it, you can't sell it."

The scepter being passed to Evelyn, Estée became free to pursue her open-ended social escalation. Still a juggernaut, jugulating all but the useful, Estée has moved beyond some of the women she once wooed with such passion in Palm Beach. Among the abandoned are Brownie McLean, daughter-in-law of Evalyn Walsh McLean, who owned the Hope Diamond. A mutual acquaintance recalled that there was a time when Estée nagged him constantly to bring Brownie around: "When Brownie's husband Jock died and Brownie began . . . to associate with a lot of people of very little importance . . . Estée dropped her . . . She's sort of forgotten about Mary [Sanford]. Mary's gotten old. And Laddie didn't leave her as much money as people thought. And it used to be that she'd call Mary and send her presents. Now she thinks the Dudleys are more social than Mary."

The Dudleys are Guilford and Chessy. He's a rich insurance man who once held an ambassadorship to Denmark under Richard Nixon. She's Chessy Dudley. They're in all the significant social registers. Estée also spends time with the Iva S. V. Patcévitches. He is the president of Condé Nast. She went to Spence. Both couples belong to the Everglades and the Bath and Tennis clubs. It is not clear what arrangements are in place at either club with respect to Estée Lauder. She is not yet included in The Palm Beach Social Register.

There was a time, after Joe's death, when she was seen with a series of "walkers"—safe and acceptable men who know their forks and make a nice appearance. One such man is still nettled. There was a time when he was escorting Estée frequently. She simply stopped returning his calls. He had done something that had angered her. Perhaps, it was that he was, quite simply, not Joe.

She used to go out with Jerry Zipkin, a man of inordinate leisure and independent means who has kept the confidences of Nancy Reagan, Betsy Bloomingdale, and Diana Vreeland. Mrs. Reagan has called him a "sort of modern-day Oscar Wilde." *Women's Wear Daily* calls him "the social moth." Zipkin is no longer evident in Estée's social life. Even at parties where he appears to be her escort, she is not photographed with him.

She is seen many places happily unescorted. She met Queen Sirikit of Thailand in March 1985, at a reception held for Her Royal Highness and an entourage of forty. It was held at Mar-A-Lago, the gigantic seaside palace where Marjorie Merriweather Post once let her large dogs run. But now Mar-A-Lago was up for sale. Sirikit and retinue were to enter through a door to receive a line of Palm Beachers, Estée among them. The Queen entered wearing a pair of golden birds whose wings fluttered when she walked. Estée wore a floral gown, floor-length—as was required of all women in Sirikit's presence in addition to wearing closed-toe shoes and not crossing their legs.

A man who has known Estée socially for more than twenty years was among the honor guard at the ceremony. He watched Estée operate in the line during the preliminary ceremonies: "Estée moved up notch by notch until she got to the very door where the queen came in," he said, "and she grabbed the queen. Estée's up there now. And there are people who have forgotten the steps she's taken. And the people in the next generation will say, 'Oh, that's Estée Lauder. She's a tough babe. She's into kings and queens now and then they won't satisfy her. Because the basic qualities aren't there.' "

There are those who see her otherwise. At Ancky Revson Johnson's villa at 190 South Ocean Road, a few doors from Estée's, in early March of 1985 (Estée was home, the guards were posted outside), the former Mrs. Revson was entertaining Princess Mary Obolensky and an English escort. Princess Obolensky organizes the backgammon tournaments in Cannes. That afternoon she and a group had played backgammon—fast and furious—on the small Formica countertop in the kitchen of the lavish villa.

Mary Obolensky is the princess who dated Leonard once or twice before his marriage to Evelyn. She talks about Estée with ebullient warmth: "I've known her since I was about twelve. And over the years I've had plenty of little problems. And I've talked to Estée. She's just sort of soft and warm and wonderful. I consider her a great friend. And I was very fond of Joe. He used to tell jokes. I think *she's* terrific. My Jewish mother!"

Ancky, with her stubborn Dutch accent and her smoky, low voice, talks about seeing Estée here and there, recently at a party for Serge of Yugoslavia. Estée was with Ancky's former husband, local realtor Ben Johnson; Ancky was with a boutique owner named Tommy de Maio. Ancky is also fond of Estée ("What she's done! Starting from nothing. I think it's fabulous."). She thinks Estée's social ambitions absurd. Ancky is not Jewish, but she prides herself on coming from a part of Europe where anti-Semitism was seldom a problem. She waves her hand with amused contempt at the thought of the Everglades Club. "If Jesus Christ himself showed up there, they *von't* let him in," she laughs.

She takes a moment to introduce two well-mannered young grandchildren. "Third-generation Revsons," she says, as though the family started with Charles.

She wonders about Estée, whose house is three, four doors away. "She's alone. I'm alone. I've no husband; she hasn't either. Sometimes I think to pick up the phone to say, 'Estée, let's get a gin game together.' Do you know what I mean? And she might be delighted. I don't know. I really don't know. It might be nice."

And she picks up the Shiny Sheet to find out where Estée was last night.

NOTES

INTRODUCTION

I learned about the "fragrant and rich" world of Estée Lauder as it has been projected in the Lauder ads by looking at the ads themselves, placed over the years in various publications. Amelia Bassin's files were enormously helpful.

It became obvious to me that the basic biographical data are barren because I scoured every available index to general and trade publications. There is only one book that includes insights and information beyond the magic: Marilyn Bender's *At the Top*, published by Doubleday in 1975. With the exception of Bender's writing, I was able to find none of the usual in-depth profiles with which a biographer usually begins to research. There simply are no gritty pieces in *Newsweek*, *Time*, *McCall's*, *The New York Times Magazine*, or *Cosmopolitan* of the kind one expects when approaching a life as noteworthy as Estée Lauder's.

The beauty tableaux cited—the quick takes about hair brushing and combing—are extrapolated from: *Women's Wear Daily*, *The Milwaukee Journal*, and Bender's always reliable *At the Top*.

The *Palm Beach Daily News* piece in which Estée claims her father was in the "social register" appeared in that newspaper on September 4, 1962.

I discovered that Estée was a "loving and dutiful daughter" through interviews with surviving tenants at the apartment house where her parents, Max and Rose Mentzer, lived for many years: 385 Fort Washington Avenue, in upper Manhattan.

I searched *The New York Times* for some kind of notice relating to the deaths of her mother and father, finding nothing. I found their names and basic birth-death information when I visited Beth-El Cemetery in New Jersey. There I knew Joe Lauder, her husband, was buried. And there I discovered the existence of other relatives of Estée's: the Rosenthal half-brothers, the Schotz connection (the family spelled the name two ways: Schatz and Schotz). With that information, and with the help of my genealogist, Laurie Thompson, I was able to obtain various documents, including death certificates and the passenger list from the ship on which her mother had first arrived in the port of New York. I knew to go to Beth-El cemetery in the first place because a Lauder family friend remembered something about Estée's people owning cemetery property in Paramus, New Jersey, where Beth-El is situated.

Jane Abbott, Director of the Oconomowoc Historical Society, worked assiduously on my behalf, obtaining information about Estée's aunt, Sarah Gottlieb. She was also helpful in delineating the history of the area. She obtained deeds, death certificates, and the little information still reposited in the memories of local people.

For written history, I used *Early Oconomowoc Heritage Trail Guidebook*, copyright 1975; Chapter 721, *Daughters of American Revolution*; and various publications of St. John's Military Academy, Delafield, Wisconsin, Archives/Museum, Nina B. Smith, Curator.

I interviewed Virginia Graham on January 29, 1985; Eileen Ryan on April 2, 1985; Lois Hagen on April 2, 1985.

BEGINNINGS

Corona and its history opened up to me through various interviews with Vincent Tomeo, a local historian who has written and lectured about the "crown community."

I found backup documentation on what it was like to live there by reading the vertical file on Corona at the Queensborough Library in Queens, New York. Corona residents spoke to me readily and pointed out the Leppel department-store connection.

Gertrude Sheldon, the daughter of Frieda Leppel, was a proud and knowledgeable source on the mercantile history of her family. I interviewed her on May 31, 1985, and again on July 18, 1985. An obituary of her mother, Frieda Plafker, which appeared on July 12, 1975, in the *Long Island Press*, was a solid historical piece that traced the store, its genesis, and the facts on Levi Leppel, after whom, Mrs. Sheldon asserts, Leonard Lauder was named.

VIENNESE WALTZ

I used standard works for my historic references to the beauty business. They included *Skin Deep*, by M. C. Phillips; *My Life for Beauty*, Helena Rubinstein; *Selling Dreams* by Margaret Allen; and *The Great American Skin Game* by Toni Stabile.

Abundant information about the life and work of John Schotz was provided to me by Lucille Carlan Rottkov. She is the keeper of that particular flame and has saved papers, passports, formulas, and pictures of her late uncle. I interviewed Mrs. Rottkov at her home in Fleischmanns, New York, on May 5, 1985. There were many follow-up telephone conversations. She also steered me to other members of her family who had worked with and known and loved Mr. and Mrs. John Schotz.

Florian Harvat told me about his recollections of Estée in Milwaukee, on April 22, 1985. I interviewed Edna Emme on March 18, 1985.

Joe Lauder's basic biographical background was revealed through birth certificates, census reports, and marriage certificates.

I had access to some of the surviving West End Avenue residents who remembered Estée during her time on West End Avenue by cross-checking Manhattan directories and reverse directories (New York residents were at one time listed according to address) with current directories. I discovered that several women who had lived in Estée's early West End Avenue apartment buildings were still there. Some remembered Estée and Joe: his early business failures, their separation, her ambition.

Several interviewees remembered that Estée sold her products at a beach club in Nassau County: one was Aida DeMaris, interviewed April 8, 1985; others were tenants in the West End Avenue apartment house were Estée lived.

SEPARATION

I was told about Uncle John's suggestion to Estée that she go to the Roney Plaza by Lucille Rottkov. Dr. John Myers's name also came up during my interview with Mrs. Rottkov. Information about John Myers I located at the Billy Rose Collection of the Lincoln Center for the Performing Arts in the Tina Louise file. And Myers's daughter, Mrs. Jeanette Vitkin, talked about her remembrances of Estée during our telephone conversation of July 15, 1985.

Estée's stopping strangers on the street is from Bender's *At the Top*: " 'I used to stop women on the street and in trains and give them tips.' She even helped a startled Salvation Army sister: 'There's no excuse for looking untidy,' she maintained."

The van Ameringen material came from various obituaries. That he was "a gentleman of the old school" was told to me by a Lauder family friend on May 8, 1985. So was Wertheimer's prediction that Estée would go far.

I talked with Sara Fredericks on June 15, 1985, and with Irma Shorell on November 7, 1984.

The fond recollections of Estee vis-à-vis the pregnant woman came to me from Diane L. Ackerman on January 24, 1985. Ackerman had attended a family funeral the same day we spoke and happened to meet up with that woman, who told Ackerman about her "dazzling smile," her "great warmth."

Robert Fiske, erstwhile cosmetics buyer at Saks Fifth Avenue, told me about Estée's abortive and then successful attempts to place her products in Saks during our telephone conversation of July 15, 1985.

Leonard remembered and related how hard his parents had worked and how long were their hours during a speech he delivered to American Women's Economic Development (AWED) on February 23, 1985. He was the first man who was asked to address that group of women executives. He also recounted the accountant's advice to his parents in the same speech.

Estée's cream vis-à-vis the skin problems of Vicki Baum and Marion Coombs was reported in *WWD*, September 12, 1969, and in Bender.

John Schotz's financial status was documented in estate forms of Anna Schotz; also by his nephew, Alan Carlan, in a telephone conversation of May 30, 1985.

YOUTH-DEW

Estée's proclamation vis-à-vis sampling was published recently in *The Miami Herald*, January 9, 1985. Asked to talk about her forthcoming autobiography, she said:

"Everyone asks me, 'How did you do it?' " Lauder says.

She won't reveal many secrets, but she says she'll write about her retailing innovations, including offering gifts with purchases. That was original in its day, although now everybody does it.

"They've copied me right down the line, even the banks."

Richard Salomon, ex-president of Charles of the Ritz, told me about that company's early experience sampling during our interview on May 30, 1985.

And Leonard Lauder talked about his parents' need to utilize sampling when he spoke to AWED, February 23, 1985.

Other important interview sources who talked about Estée's selling, hawking, and standing behind counters included Agnes Ash, February 27, 1985; Bob Wirtz, January 28, 1985; Harry Doyle, May 16, 1985; Don Viall, March 14, 1985.

I learned about Van Venneri's background and her relationship with the up-and-coming Estée Lauder through various clippings in *WWD* and during my talks with Harry Doyle. Virginia Graham told me about her cousin, Gladys Hyman, and how Hyman helped Estée in Marshall Field.

The friend of Estée's who talked to me about Sally' Freed's castigation on Estée's Jewishness chose not to be named in my book. I interviewed her on April 15, 1985, and reconfirmed Freed's remarks, as she remembered them, the next day.

Andrew Lucarelli spoke about his early experiences working for Lauder and compared Youth-Dew to Giorgio in our interview of December 11, 1984.

THE BEGINNING OF THE BEGINNING

Leonard's behavior as a young, nervous, out-to-prove-himself executive and his lack of interest in how he dressed were described to me in informative, face-to-face interviews with two men who worked for the Lauder company then and have since gone on to high-level positions in other cosmetic companies. They are Anthony Liebler of Paco-Rabanne and Andrew Lucarelli, who is now with Revlon. I talked with Liebler on May 29, 1985, and again on June 10, 1985; Lucarelli was interviewed on December 11, 12, and 18, 1984.

That Leonard Lauder referred to his mother as "Mrs. Lauder" was cited in Bender. Mrs. Lauder would begin, at a later time, to refer to herself as "Mrs. Lauder." She was quoted by Diane Sustendal, *The Times-Picayune*, July 18, 1982: " 'Tell your readers that Mrs. Lauder says whenever they are tired or pale they should use coral blush very close to the eyes.' "

Leonard's assertion that "She is the company; the company is she" comes from a *Vogue* profile of January 1973.

Jean Baer's informal notes to herself, which she took along when she went to interview Leonard Lauder, were shown to me by Mrs. Baer during our interview on January 14, 1985.

Andrew Lucarelli discussed Estée's and Leonard's different attitudes as he perceived them toward their Jewishness during our interviews. Lucarelli told me: with reference to his early experiences working at the offices of Estée Lauder, Inc. when I asked him to talk about the subject of Estée's observances: "It never came up. But the *fact* that it never came up? It was like holidays. He [Leonard] would take off, but she was always 'away'."

Andrew Lucarelli explained Ira Levy's relationship to Estée during our interview; he also recounted the episode of the Christmas card.

Two fine books, *Fire and Ice* by Andrew Tobias, and *Madame* by Patrick O'Higgins, provided me with good insights into those other entrepreneurs. The story of Estée's avoiding competing with Revson by producing a competitive nail polish was told by Leonard in his speech before AWED.

I interviewed Mary Sanford on March 4, 1985, and Lois Hagen on April 9, 1985.

I interviewed the press agent who described Palm Beach as "one wonderful round big ball," on March 5, 1985. The other press agent, who described Estée's house on Route Trail and her better "creamy villa," I talked to on February 7, 1985.

Estée's bold solicitation to be asked to the George Vigoreux fete was told to me by yet another press agent on January 21, 1985.

Background information on the social history of that community came from the files of the *Palm Beach Daily News*; *The New York Times*, January 30, 1964: "Palm Beach in Winter" by Charlotte Curtis; *Esquire*, January 1970: "Poor Little Palm Beach" by Stephen Birmingham; *Newsweek*, November 21, 1966: "The Best Place"; *The New York Times*, "Palm Beach: An Immutable Social Bastion" by Marilyn Bender; *Time*, February 10, 1961: "Playgrounds"; *Town & Country*, November 1970: "Florida's Gold Coast" by Ted Burke.

REVSON'S FOLLY

Madame Rubinstein's robbery was recounted in Patrick O'Higgins's *Madame*. And that her company's products were "sold like soap" is from author interview with Robert Kramer, February 8, 1985. He said: "Look at Rubinstein when the old lady died. Colgate tried to sell it like soap and it went to pieces."

The confusion about Elizabeth Arden's age came from *The New York Times* obituary on Arden: "Mrs. Graham's age has been a mystery during her life, but a representative of Elizabeth Arden, Inc., of which she was chairman of the board and president, said yesterday that she was 81 years old. The spokesman gave the birth date as December 31, 1884. Others had placed Mrs. Graham's age closer to 84."

Revson's background was primarily taken from *Fire and Ice*; Estée's articulations were explained to me by Tony Liebler on May 29, 1985. Revson's railings that Estée was really "Esther-from-Brooklyn" were experienced by and relayed to me by Harry Doyle.

Estée's attempt to board the train with the Windsors came from an anonymous source, March 6, 1985.

The Revson-Lauder rivalry was chronicled in: *Palm Beach Daily News*, September 5, 1976, lead article by Agnes Ash; *WWD*, February 13, 1970, "The War of the Rosebuds"; *WWD*, "The War of the Roses," September 26, 1969.

I learned about the cachet of the Duke and Duchess of Windsor in *The Woman He Loved*, by Ralph G. Martin, and *The Windsor Story*, by Charles Murphy. Newspaper articles include: *The New York Times*, "The Windsors in International Society," May 29, 1972, by Charlotte Curtis.

Marilyn Bender wrote her story of how Estée met the Duchess in *At the Top*: "Mrs. Lauder says she met the Windsors on an Atlantic crossing of the S.S. *United States*. According to her version, the Duchess said she wanted to meet her because she had been using Estée Lauder products for ages. The Duke said that Youth-Dew was the only fragrance he liked. They had cocktails together and the friendship ripened in Palm Beach, Paris, and other points distant from West End Avenue."

CLINIQUE

Andrew Lucarelli, who was there, talked to me about the Skrebneski picture of Phyllis Connor and Leonard's response to it, December 12, 1984. And June Leaman commented on what the Lauder woman was supposed to represent in a Lauder company pamphlet called *21 Years of Estée Lauder Photography by Skrebneski*.

The conversation between Estée and Carol Phillips at lunch was related to me by a Clinique employee to whom Phillips told the story, January 31, 1985. Information about Clinique and its uniqueness came from *What the Ads Don't Tell You* by Carol Rinzler. The biographical background of Phillips came from a profile of her in *Cosmopolitan*, November 1980.

I garnered facts about Irving Penn from his file at the Museum of Modern Art; *Vogue*, September 1980, September 1982, and September 1984.

The history of earlier hypo-allergenic products was detailed in *Drug & Cosmetic*, May 1958. The company's sales figures appeared in an issue of *Advertising Age*, February 26, 1979.

That Clinique lost money was recounted by Bender, quoting Leonard: " 'If we had been public, I would never have launched Clinique. . . . We took a bath before it started paying off.' "

Clinique sales figures were cited in *Advertising Age*, February 26, 1979.

QUEEN ESTÉE

Harry Doyle was there when Estée and Revson met in the elevator. He told me about their confrontation and Revson's "thin" smile, May 16, 1985.

Estée's house in the south of France and her description of how she used the air to inspire a fragrance were described in *W*, September 16–23, 1977; "Estée Lauder: Enjoying a Change of Air," by Edwina LaFarge. She told Bender in *At the Top* that she wanted to live in the south of France: "as formally as in New York." Nina Schick, on June 18, 1985, talked to me about arranging Estée's flowers.

My readings about Mrs. Gould included *The New York Times*, March 17, 1983; *The New York Times*, November 29, 1984; *New York Post*, March 20, 1985; *New York Post*, April 25, 1985.

The story about Estée's reaction to seeing her friend the Begum as the flashbulbs popped was told to me by a friend who was there in an interview on May 1, 1985.

One of Estée's other social friends, who was at the party for the opening of the film about the Duke, told me about Rose Kennedy, December 8, 1984. And Estée's interview about friendship appeared in the *Palm Beach Daily News*, October 12, 1969: "After a Fashion" by Marian Christy.

A press agent who was in Palm Beach during the betel-nut box delivery told me about the incident on February 7, 1985, and about what her George Washington Day birthday parties were like. And another Palm Beach savant talked to me about the division between Jewish and non-Jewish friends. The first press agent, who told me about the betel-nut box, also related the response of the other hostess on being invited to Estée's B parties.

The friendship between Estée and designer Jo Copeland has been described to me by several people who knew them both. I tried very hard to convince Copeland's daughter, Lois Gould, to chat with me, but she refused. But the Copeland name came up in several interviews; the two women had presumably been very close. As to Copeland's reported resentment at feeling that she was being segregated, one anonymous source said: "She [Jo] always resented the fact that Estée kept her separate. She did not put her together with her ritzy friends." Another mutual friend told me: "I think she [Jo] knew Estée for what she was. I think there were the A parties and the B parties, and I don't think toward the end Jo was invited to the A parties."

Estée's nun story came to me from three different sources. An ex-employee of Estée's told me that he met that ecclesiastic when he was at work one day: "I was in somebody's office and she brought in a nun and she introduced the nun as her cousin." I asked the source if the nun had a habit on; he answered that she did. I asked him how Estée introduced her. He replied that Estée said: " 'This is my cousin, Sister . . .' "

A Palm Beach–New York press agent told me: "She has a niece or a cousin who's a Roman Catholic nun. She had this nun come and stay with her in Palm Beach and go to parties."

When I interviewed Gertrude Sheldon, who is a daughter of Frieda Leppel, Gertrude remembered going to a party years before for a relative of Estée's. Sheldon told me, on July 18, 1985: "There was a Sister, an unmarried woman. . . . She went into the nunnery. . . . The nun was a cousin of Estée's: a Jewish lady who converted to Catholicism. I don't know her name. I don't know if she is still living."

The Everglades Club and its membership policy have been the subject of several recent news pieces, largely on account of the New York City Ballet's refusal to party on their premises because the club does not admit Jews as members. That particular incident was reported in *The Miami Herald*, March 23, 1985: "N.Y.C. Ballet gives Everglades Club the boot," by Mike Wilson. Wilson wrote, "The historic Everglades Club, 356

Worth Avenue, has long been known for its refusal to admit Jews as members or guests." The Palm Beach *Jewish World*, March 29–April 4, 1985, contained a piece called "No ballet at the Everglades" by David Bittner. Bittner wrote: "The Everglades Club, which has a policy against admitting Jews as members or even guests . . ." And Stephen Birmingham in *Our Crowd* refers to "the elite Christian Everglades Club."

Estée's own incident at the club with Mrs. Guest was confirmed by many people, including those quoted in text: Agnes Ash, Charlotte Curtis, James Brady, various local press agents, Mary Sanford. The whole episode has taken on an almost folklorish quality in the Palm Beach community. Everybody knows it happened. People still speak of it.

Estée's response on the issue was printed in *The Miami Herald*, April 8, 1985, page 12: "Private Clubs: A World Apart."

Marvin Davis, the advertising man who wrote the letter to Ronald about "the fey schmuck" on the pool table, told me about Estée's observance of Passover. We talked on November 16, 1984. Davis was repeating a story told to him by his cousin, Ira Levy. Levy had been there. Levy claimed to have seen Estée in her hoover apron routing *chometz*. And a Jewish, Yiddish-speaking man, who was a friend of the family and escorted Estée for a time after Joe's death, told me about her speaking Yiddish and doing so occasionally when she was with him.

Harry Doyle told me the story of Joe telephoning New York, looking for an excuse to leave Palm Beach. The story had been told to him by Leonard Lauder.

The quote about Estée being "a real Jewish mama" came from a former Rubinstein employee during our interview, April 11, 1985.

LISTEN TO YOUR CUSTOMERS

I listened to Leonard's speech before AWED, which is how I know his voice was reedy and affable.

The basic differences between marketing approaches, sell-in vs. sell-thru, were explained to me over a long lunch interview with Anthony Liebler, who was with Lauder and opening accounts on their behalf in the early days. The interview with Liebler was on June 10, 1985.

The Neiman-Marcus executive was interviewed on May 1, 1985; he also added to Liebler's account of the dynamics of department-store selling: charge-backs, commissions, etc.

Richard Salomon, past president of Charles of the Ritz, told me about Leonard's planning mechanisms and how innovative he has been over the years. Salomon is a tremendous admirer of Leonard's as a businessman and as a person.

If Estée indicates that her contribution to the creation of a fragrance begins in the laboratory, she is not alone among cosmetics entrepreneurs. Writing about the subject of IFF and the secrecy in the fragrance business, Lee Smith wrote in *Fortune*, August 9, 1962, "Adventures in the Sex and Hunger Trade": "The mystery [of the fragrance business] is compounded by a code of discretion that protects the customers. The sex and hunger industry makes most of the smells and tastes that are used by cosmetic and food companies, aromas from couturier perfume to furniture polish. . . . For the most part the companies would prefer the ultimate consumer to believe that all those distinctive smells and tastes were invented on their own premises—that is, those of Revlon, Estée Lauder, or General Foods. Some actually are. The houses of Chanel and Gerlain in Paris make all their own perfume." The article continues with some comments from Hercules Segalas: "Hercules Segalas, who was an IFF and P&G executive before joining Drexel Burnham, believes that 20 big customers account for close to half of IFF's sales. The largest,

Segalas thinks, is Unilever, followed by a group that includes Estée Lauder, Colgate, P&G, Pepsico, and General Foods."

Estée's "nose" was discussed by several of my interviewees, including an erstwhile Fabergé executive, who is now a consultant in the field of fragrance: . . . "I think she was going to say that they were all made under her direction. And, in a way, all of them were. You say what you like and what you don't like. She may have a very good 'nose,' but she did not blend the perfume. I have a picture of her where she's standing in a white coat and looking like a perfumer. . . . She may well have a fine, consumer-type nose, *but*!"

Allan Mottus talked to me about Estée's perfectionism—her recalling the imperfect fragrance, May 26, 1985; Amelia Bassin commented during my interview with her, "I remember when Opium first came out . . ." on October 30, 1984.

Estée told *WWD* that she almost passed out at seeing Opium: September 22, 1978.

The Cinnabar-Opium competition attracted a great deal of industry attention because such competitive behavior among giants is dramatic and fun. So there was much to read, including: *Cosmetic World*, October 2, 1979, "Lauder Soft on Opium"; *Advertising Age*, October 9, 1979; *The New York Times*, June 5, 1979; *The New York Times*, "Success and a Bit of Controversy, at $100 an Ounce," December 18, 1978; *The Wall Street Journal*, February 5, 1980; *The New York Times*, "France vs US," August 5, 1979; *Advertising Age*, May 21, 1979; and other stories in *Product Marketing*.

The *WWD* piece in which Ronald is quoted extensively vis-à-vis his mother and her creation of Soft Youth-Dew and/or Cinnabar was "Lauder's Cinnabar exudes Oriental mystique," *WWD*, September 15, 1978, by Joan Harting.

POUR L'HOMME

I read various articles about Karen Graham, among them *New York Post*, March 8, 1978; *Life*, October 1981; and *W*, October 14, 1974. June Leaman's comments on the targeting of the Lauder market in print appeared in an undated issue of *Madison Avenue Magazine*, which I found in the files of Amelia Bassin.

A Lauder company spokeswoman told *Advertising Age*, February 28, 1983, that women were responsible for 76–77 percent of their sales of men's fragrances.

Three useful articles on the history of men's fragrances were: *The New York Times*, June 10, 1978, "Smelling Good Costly for Men"; *Working Woman*, November 1982, "What Smell Success?" by Julia Kagan; *Drug & Cosmetic*, February 1978, "Devin Aramis Country Fragrance," Catherine Hunter.

That Leonard and Estée were furious with George Friedman came to me from two sources. Marvin Davis told me, on November 16, 1984, "When Friedman was wooed away by Steve Ross, the Lauders stopped talking to him." An anonymous source asserted in a mid-May 1985 telephone conversation, "Leonard never forgave him [meaning Friedman]."

The Ruttenberg-Revlon story was related by a friend of Ruttenberg's on February 14, 1985.

The story about Joseph LaRosa and the man in the box was told to me by LaRosa, November 21, 1984. I spoke to the other ad man, Marvin Davis, who tried unsuccessfully to create an image for Aramis, on November 16, 1984. Davis told me about the lunch at "21," about Ronald offending Attardi by leaving the room, about the note Ira Levy sent to him commenting on Ronald's behavior, about the sky-writing attempt that never came off. He also commented on Leonard's behavior.

The Aramis campaign under AC&R was chronicled in *The New York Times*, October 12, 1981, "Meetings"; Lou Miano's ebullient speech was cited in Amelia Bassin's column "Bird's Eye View";

and in *Drug & Cosmetic*, September 1983. I took the general background of AC&R from *The New York Times*, May 8, 1981, and March 12, 1981.

The history of Revson's half-hearted attempt to get social like Estée was revealed in my interview with Ancky Johnson, March 2, 1985, and in Andrew Tobias's *Fire and Ice*, "The Story of Charles Revson—the Man Who Built the Revlon Empire."

GIFT WITH PURPOSE

The robbery at Estée's house was covered extensively in the New York press. My sources there included: New York *Daily News*, October 17, 1979. There are two stories in two editions: "Handcuff Estée Lauder, grab 31G in cash, gems"; "3 rob Estée Lauder of 1M at home." The *News* followed up on October 18, 1979, "Cops comb Estée Lauder townhouse for heist clues." *New York Post* ran a front-page story on October 17, 1979, "Million-Dollar Riddle of Estée Lauder."

Agnes Ash told me on February 27, 1985, that Estée was frightened during the robbery.

Several sources told me about Estée's security precautions since the robbery. In fact, I saw the guards outside her Palm Beach house when I passed in my car; and I saw the protruding television cameras attached to her New York mansion. They were winking at me.

The information about her various honors I garnered from a host of pieces in the *New York Post*, January 18, 1978; *Daily News*, January 18, 1978; *Newsweek*, February 6, 1978; *The New York Times*, January 18, 1978; *WWD*, April 7, 1978. Joe's remark, "I'm not going to carry your bags," appeared in *WWD*, January 7, 1983, "Estée and Joe."

I interviewed the Duchess's former secretary on January 22, 1985; information about the Duchess's health comes from Charles Murphy's *The Windsor Story*.

The parties Estée gave for Princess Grace were widely reported. I learned about them from an article by Eugenia Sheppard that begins, "Who BUT Estée Lauder would think of bringing a Salvation Army band indoors at her East Side townhouse to play Christmas songs," *Palm Beach Daily News*, November 2, 1978; *WWD*, December 15, 1980, in article starting, "It was Estée and Joe Lauder's Christmas party for the Princesses and the Ladies."

An anonymous source who entertained the Spencers told me

that Lord Spencer had complained, to her, about Joe's bold request. The interview was on January 22, 1985. Allan Mottus told me that Estée was afraid that the Prince would fall off his horse, March 27, 1985. Details of the Queen's own fears for Prince Charles were reported in *Royal Service: My Twelve Years as Valet to Prince Charles*, Stephen P. Barry, published in 1983 by Macmillan.

I found a wide variety of reportage on The Estée and Joe Lauder Foundation in the vertical file of the Foundation available at The Foundation Center, 79 Fifth Avenue, New York. The Foundation figures I cite all come from tax returns that are reposited at the Foundation Center. Tax returns of foundations are public record. The article about the women's group that criticized the cosmetics companies is from *Mother Jones*, a magazine, and can be found in the Lauder vertical file at the Foundation Center. That article includes the Revson executive's dismissive reaction.

An anonymous philanthropist told me that Estée was a canny giver; the Neiman-Marcus executive on May 1, 1985, talked about Estée's selfishness.

Ronald's museum party was reported in *The New York Times*, October 3, 1981, "And With Mailed Fist Raise a Toast."

I learned about Estée's television habits in *WWD*, January 7, 1983, "Estée and Joe"; her taking the grandchildren to polo matches and changing in the south of France from Diane L. Ackerman, October 29, 1984.

Estée's breakfast habits were published in a profile that appeared in the *Sun-Sentinel*, June 5, 1981: "Estée Lauder: The reigning queen in the world of beauty and fragrance." Writer Genevieve Buck is identified as a *Chicago Tribune* reporter.

Estée's remark to her executive, "Your children don't need you now," was told to me during an interview with him on February 14, 1985.

All the stories about La Reserve, Estée's cruising the room, and the property in the south of France being too expensive for growing flowers were told to me by a social friend of the Lauders.

Estée's claim about speaking French was reported in *WWD*'s "Estée and Joe"; a friend of hers who spent a good deal of time with the Lauders in the south of France told me that Estée does not speak French, that her maid serves Ritz crackers.

Joe's "toleration" of Estée's social peregrinations were reported to me by virtually every source available.

I talked to the woman who had queried Estée about why the company did not do business with Israel on April 15, 1985. Her employer told me about a conversation he had overheard on another occasion between that woman and Estée. He said that Estée "pulled back" when the conversation got too ethnic; the woman herself told me about Estée's discussion about selling to Israel.

The list of companies boycotted by Arabs was published in *The Arab Blacklist Unveiled* by Edward Hotaling. Copies of that booklet are available at The American Jewish Committee, 165 East 56th Street, New York, NY 10022.

Allan Mottus told me during our interview of May 26, 1985: "To be going to Israel after all these other companies are already there—from a business point of view, I don't think they [Lauder] had many options. . . . Her fragrances apparently do very well in the Middle East: they do like those heavier, pungent fragrances."

Estée was cited, namely her new fragrance, "It will come. I'll think of it," in *Sun-Sentinel*, June 5, 1981, by Genevieve Buck.

J.H.L.

Estée's reasons for creating J.H.L. and Ira Levy's comments and descriptions of how the fragrance package was based on Joe's own habiliments were all contained in *W*, October 8–15, 1982, "JHL: For Joe, from Estée," by Pete Born. Ira was referred to as Estée's "dauphin" during my interview with Marvin Davis on November 16, 1984. The launching at Harrods and Saks is from *Working Woman*, November 1982, "What Smell Success?" by Julia Kagan.

The incident at the Colony restaurant, the fact that Estée had reserved a room in a different hotel under the wife's name, was told to me by the wife, during a telephone interview of March 24, 1985.

Harry Doyle told me about Joe and his glass of scotch on May 16, 1985.

Diane L. Ackerman told me that Joe's face lit up when he looked at Estée, January 23, 1985. His wry humor, as exemplified by "I'm glad you did, we need the business," appeared in *WWD*, "Estée and Joe." That was a nice, warm, and rather candid piece that appeared a week before Joe's death. His one expression of temper came from an anonymous source who was there.

The business statistics globally appeared in *WWD*, "Selling of Estée Lauder," April 17, 1982.

Estée told *The New York Times*, "I'm the only one left," April 18, 1982, "Estée Lauder: The Scents of Success" by Sandra Salmans. And I learned that Lauder used foreign labs in *BusinessWeek*, September 26, 1983, "Lauder's Success Formula: Instinct, Timing, and Research."

The piece about *Prescriptives* and Mrs. Lauder's nettlesomely superior products came from *The Sunday Times*, London, September 28, 1980, by Mary Davis Peters. The business bottom-lines cited right after are from *W*, "JHL: For Joe, from Estée."

Savvy magazine, November 1984, ran a piece about Aspen from which I quoted; Leonard's reaction to China trip in *WWD*, November 19, 1982.

Ronald's political aspirations and activities came from articles that included *WWD*, February 25, 1983; *The New York Times*, "On the Job Training at the Pentagon," August 19, 1983. *The Washington Post* piece, "Cosmetic Executive for Defense Job?" appeared November 10, 1982.

The details of Joe's death were from various primary sources. Particularly useful was Eugenia Sheppard's featured article that appeared in the *New York Post* on January 17, 1983. I was advised by Marilyn Bender to look for that piece. Bender criticized the obituary that had run in her own newspaper, *The New York Times*. She told me, during a telephone interview, January 29, 1985: "That [the *Times's* obituary] was a perfectly terrible obit. It sounded as if Lauder's flack had personally written it. Good old Eugenia had the better story in the *Post*. She was the one who spelled out where he was buried."

Harry Doyle told me about his meeting Estée at the theater during our telephone conversation of July 31, 1985. The Robert Ruttenberg story was told to me by a friend of Ruttenberg's on February 14, 1985.

BEYOND THE MAGIC

Ronald was quoted in *The New York Times*, "On the Job Training at the Pentagon." And LaRosa spoke to me about his own response to Ronald's having a Pentagon position during our meeting on November 21, 1984. An anonymous source assessed Ronald's political ambitions to me on January 31, 1985.

The Kirkpatrick-Lauder encounter was reported in *WWD*, "Eye," January 22, 1985.

Estée's "How does a cream know it's dark outside?" came from Bender's *At the Top*.

Dr. Norman Orentreich's comment about topical preparations appeared in *Drug & Cosmetic*, September 1984. And Dr. Albert M. Kligman made his comments to me during a telephone interview of June 15, 1985.

Dr. Barbara Gilchrest's assertions were published originally in *How a Woman Ages*, Robin Marantz Henig and the Editors of Esquire Magazine, Ballantine, 1985.

Drs. Novack and Greewald's comments to Betty Furness I took from a transcript of NBC's *Today*, Thursday, June 27, 1985. I spoke with Furness about why she did that segment on July 11, 1985.

The *Essence* spokesperson and I had a telephone interview on July 31, 1985. I interviewed Amelia Bassin on the subject of the black-skin market and the racist schism in cosmetic advertising, July 31, 1985.

The Warner-L'Oréal-Cosmair network is a labyrinthine phenomenon. I read various pieces about its history and formation. Those pieces included: *Cosmetic Insiders' Report*, January 9, 1984, and February 18, 1984; *The New York Times*, May 21, 1985, "Cosmair Makes a Name for Itself"; *The Informationist*, January 1984; *Forbes*, March 12, 1984, "On the Scent"; *The Wall Street Journal*, March 9, 1984; *The New York Times*, April 9, 1982.

I spoke to various people in the industry about Warner vis-à-vis Lauder: Don Davis of *Cosmetic Insiders' Report*, February 4, 1985; Allan Mottus, industry consultant and publisher of *The Informationist*, May 26, 1985. And the Warner executive on February 14, 1985.

Allan Mottus told me during our interview on May 26, 1985, about his experiences with Estée and Leonard when Mottus hurt his leg during our interview on May 26, 1985.

The Lauder for Men luncheon was also discussed during my talk with Mottus. He had attended. Another useful account appeared in *New York*, May 13, 1985.

Estée's relationship with Brownie McLean and Mary Sanford was discussed during an interview with an anonymous Palm Beach source, March 7, 1985; so, too, was her friendship with the Dudleys and the Patcévitches.

Jerry Zipkin sources included the *Daily News*, November 25, 1980. Writer Jennifer Allen began her story, "Nancy Reagan has a walker . . ."; *People*, December 7, 1981; *The New York Times*, January 19, 1985, "Second Time Around Inaugural Parties Glitter."

Activities of Estée at the fete for Queen Sirikit told to me by anonymous Palm Beach sources, March 6 and March 7, 1985. I used reportage that included: *New York Post*, March 12, 1985, "Around the Town" by Amy Penn; *Palm Beach Daily News*, March 7, 1985, "Thai Queen Tells About Her People," Baroness Garnett Stackelberg.

I interviewed Ancky Johnson at her home in Palm Beach on March 2, 1985. Mary Obolensky, who was visiting that day, sat and commented about her fond feelings for Estée.

INDEX

177